OCCUPATIONAL MOBILITY

IN THE UNITED STATES

1930-1960

OCCUPATIONAL MOBILITY
IN THE UNITED STATES
1930-1960

A. J. JAFFE

R. O. CARLETON

With a Preface by Seymour L. Wolfbein

KING'S CROWN PRESS

Columbia University, New York, 1954

Library of Congress Catalog Card Number: 54-11813

Published in Great Britain, Canada, India, and Pakistan
by Geoffrey Cumberlege, Oxford University Press
London, Toronto, Bombay, and Karachi

MANUFACTURED IN THE UNITED STATES OF AMERICA

PREFACE

Considering the significant needs for information on patterns of working life
- for the working population as a whole as well as for individual occupations - surprisingly little research has been carried on in this field. To a great extent our thinking on this subject has consisted of an uneasy composite of two contradictory legends or stereotypes: first, the assumption (all too common in vocational guidance) that people choose an occupation, train for it, enter it, progress in it and in due time retire from it; second, the Horatio Alger tradition - from shoeshine boy to bank president in regulation time.

The realities behind these legends are relevant to a number of problem areas in addition to the general light they may shed on the sociology of work. In the appraisal of manpower requirements and supply for a mobilization economy it is essential to be able to assess the flexibility and occupational mobility of workers. In estimating the long-term employment outlook as a basis for determining the size of vocational training or educational programs, data are necessary on the prospective losses to each occupation resulting from retirement or the movement of workers to other occupations. In reviewing the content and goals of educational programs and providing a context for vocational guidance, an understanding of the patterns of working life and the kinds of occupational changes people make are extremely valuable.

Dr. Jaffe's and Mr. Carleton's contribution to the recently growing literature in this field is especially significant because it is a pioneer attempt to study mobility and patterns of working life by applying cohort analysis to the data from successive decennial censuses of population. What they have accomplished on the study of major occupation groups points a clear way for further analysis of individual occupations. Finally not the least of the contributions of this study is the ingenious and painstaking work required in adjusting the Census data to make them comparable from one census to another for purposes of analysis. Everyone interested in the varied aspects of working life patterns owes Dr. Jaffe and Mr. Carleton a debt of gratitude for this volume.

Seymour L. Wolfbein

FOREWORD

This project was undertaken with a very specific goal in mind, namely, the construction of models and procedures for estimating possible future manpower supply by occupation in the United States.[1] These were the terms of reference laid down in the original study outline and adhered to throughout the study.

During the process of actually building these models and applying them to data, considerable additional information was obtained on certain aspects of mobility directly associated with changes in occupational distribution. It is believed that these data are significant enough in their own right to warrant separate presentation, and accordingly this is being done. However, in light of the purpose of this project primary emphasis in our report is being placed upon the models and the data relating to the projection of manpower supply by occupation; such projections were calculated for 1960 for the total male population of the United States and are shown in Part I. Secondarily, we are presenting such additional information and derivative analyses as were obtained bearing on: (a) the rate of new entries into major occupation groups, (b) retirements by occupations, (c) net mobility among the various occupations, and (d) patterns of working life. These analyses are presented in Part II. Our methodology is described in Part III.

Furthermore, in view of the main purpose of the project it should be emphasized that:

1. We are concerned with occupational mobility exclusively; all other types of labor mobility receive secondary, if any, consideration in this report;

2. Projection rather than historical analysis was the dominant consideration.

As will be developed in more detail subsequently, any changes in the basic purpose of the study would have resulted in changes in the models and procedures which would have led ultimately to a study very different from that presented here.

Occupational mobility is but one aspect of labor mobility. Other aspects include mobility among industries, mobility among employers, geographic mobility, change between status of employed and unemployed, etc. Perhaps the most comprehensive definition of labor mobility would involve the sum totality of all factors which describe how a person earns his livelihood throughout his lifetime.[2]

Obviously the occupation which he enters or his movements from one occupation to another or the occupation from which he retires are but a part of the story. Other parts have been studied and described in various other publications to which the reader is referred. One such volume is Herbert S. Parnes, "Research on Labor Mobility: An Appraisal of Research Findings in the United States," Social Science Research Council Bulletin 65, 1954; another is Gladys L. Palmer, Labor Mobility in Six Cities, Social Science Research Council, 1954; still another is Mobility and Economic Opportunity, Technology Press and John Wiley and Sons, 1954.

Our study on occupational mobility and the above-mentioned studies supplement each other to a considerable extent. We have gone into certain aspects of occupational

---

1. "This research was supported in whole or in part by The United States Air Force under Contract No. AF 18(600)-654, monitored by Deputy Chief of Staff, Comptroller, Headquarters, USAF, AFAPA-3E, Washington 25, D. C."

2. See Gladys Palmer, Labor Mobility in Six Cities, Social Science Research Council, New York, 1954, Chapter 1, "Why Study Mobility." See also Herbert S. Parnes, "Research on Labor Mobility," Social Science Research Council Bulletin 65, New York, 1954, Chapter 2, "Some Conceptual and Methodological Problems."

mobility to a considerably greater extent than have these other studies. On the other hand, these other studies have investigated other aspects of labor mobility - aspects which we ignored almost entirely in our study.

Since the main purpose of this study was to project the occupational composition of the male civilian adult population of the United States, all of the models and the calculations were designed and carried through for projection purposes. This means in turn that they are less useful for describing the purely historical picture. If the aim of our study had been to ascertain historically what happened in the United States and without making any attempt to project into the future, we would have built somewhat different models and would have carried out different types of calculations. As will be seen in the discussion of the methodology, Part III, we adopted these procedures which were most pertinent for providing an estimate of the future occupational distribution. Subsequently in attempting to analyze the derived information for substantive findings of a historical nature, we must confess that such history has not always been clearly demarked. In various situations, perhaps most obviously in the case of new entries, a better historical picture would have resulted from the use of different procedures. As mentioned in the methodological discussion, however, such other procedures as might have been used would not have permitted making projections of the new entries in the decade 1950 to 1960.

We also were not directly concerned with an analysis of the factors in the society - social, economic, demographic, cultural, technological and other factors - which influence the changes in occupational composition. Considerable discussion of the historical roles of many of these factors will be found in the volume Manpower Resources and Utilization by A. J. Jaffe and Charles D. Stewart. The present study makes some use of the information available about the changes in the social scene which have accompanied the observed occupational changes. We have not, however, tried to bring in new evidence on these interrelationships nor to investigate them in any great detail.

In order to obtain more information on life patterns of occupational mobility than was possible from the analysis of census data alone, additional materials from the Six City Study were utilized. A special tabulation of the original cards was designed, and this tabulation was made by the United States Census Bureau. On the basis of these data we calculated working life patterns, showing the occupations which youth entered at the beginning of their working careers cross-classified by the occupations they held at the end of their careers. The results show the extent of movement up and down the occupational ladder. These life patterns together with related materials are presented in Chapter 7.

The authors wish to thank the following members of the Committee which helped set the framework for this study: David Kaplan, Margaret Martin, Gladys Palmer, Robert Steffes, Col. Watson and Seymour L. Wolfbein. We also wish to express our appreciation to the United States Census Bureau for guidance on the problems of reclassifying census data and for making available to us advance tabulations from the 1950 Census. To Miss Edith Donald we express our thanks for editing and typing the manuscript. Although we are happy to acknowledge the advice and aid received from friends and colleagues - including those whose names we may have inadvertently omitted - we alone assume full responsibility for the quality and quantity of this investigation.

Bureau of Applied Social Research
Columbia University
June, 1954   A. J. Jaffe
                                                    R. C. Carleton

TABLE OF CONTENTS

Part I. Problem and Summary of Findings

Part II. The Components of Change

Part III. Methodology

TABLES

TABLES

CHARTS

CHAPTER 1
INTRODUCTION

Aim of Project

From time to time research efforts have been directed at attempts to estimate manpower requirements in the United States under hypothesized conditions. Simultaneously it has been recognized that such possible requirements cannot be understood or evaluated without reference to possible supply.

Furthermore it is recognized that neither requirements nor supply are uniquely determinable for the simple reason that under varying conditions both can be increased or decreased. For example, even the total United States population does not set an ultimate ceiling on manpower supply since under certain conditions (theoretically, if not actually, conceivable) the United States can draw upon the manpower resources of other parts of the Western Hemisphere.

This range of variation in possible size of manpower supply has long been recognized by students of the subject. Accordingly efforts have been directed at trying to estimate the manpower which might be required and which might be available under certain specified conditions. When specifying the conditions, it then becomes possible to speak in much more definite terms than would be the case if we simply tried to speak of manpower in some broad generalized manner.

This particular study is concerned with the manpower supply situation in the United States. It is limited to males and covers the decades 1930 to 1960. The basic question considered here is: on the basis of our knowledge of changes in male manpower supply in the decades 1930 to 1950, how might we go about extrapolating this past history into the future - say a decade hence into 1960. The answer to this question as it is developed in this monograph involves specific assumptions regarding a whole host of conditions which might be encountered during the 1950s.

The most basic assumption necessary, which must be emphasized at the outset, is that conditions in the 1950s will be substantially "normal" in the sense that there will be no repetition of World War II in the years ahead to 1960. We are extrapolating "normal" past history into a "normal" future in an effort to estimate the characteristics of the "normal" supply of civilian male workers which might be available. If highly "abnormal" conditions are to be posited, such as those involved in large-scale warfare, then the characteristics of this labor supply may be altered beyond recognition. In such an event the extrapolation of past history becomes almost a game of chance.

Development of models. "Model cohort work experience tables" were designed for the major occupational groups as presented in the United States decennial censuses of population for the periods 1930 to 1950. The primary purpose of these models was to devise a framework which would permit uncovering: (1) the net occupational mobility which actually occurred during these twenty years; (2) the occupational distribution of new entrants into the labor force during the 1930s and during the 1940s; and (3) the occupational distribution of retirements from the labor force in each of these decades. The actual models were so constructed that they could be applied to any number of occupations and any type of occupational classification scheme which might be available or desired. These models were built to be applied to males only, mainly because of methodological considerations. It is believed that similar models could be developed for women also but that of necessity they would have to be much more complex than the ones for men.

In developing the models, the major emphasis was placed on practicality. The intent was to develop models which could be applied meaningfully and practically and which at the same time would be logically and technically sound. No attempt was made to try to develop highly complex models requiring types of data which are at present unavailable and which are likely to be unavailable in the immediate future. In short all the emphasis was placed on building models which could be put into use at present.

Application of the models. As part of the process of developing these models and insuring their practicality, we tested them with data continuously and modified them as necessary in view of the limitations of the available data. Consequently the results presented in this volume are the joint product of theoretical model-building and application to existing data.

In developing and testing these models, they were applied to the United States population census data on major occupational distribution (i.e., ten major groups) for males, for the censuses of 1930, 1940 and 1950. We then made projections of the ten major occupational groups to 1960, for the males. These projections involve estimates of the numbers and occupational distribution of new entries into the labor force in the decade 1950 to 1960, estimates of net occupational mobility, estimates of the numbers of retirements from the labor force by occupation during this decade, and estimates of the amount of mortality which might be expected.

Altogether four sets of estimates were prepared. Methodologically and from the viewpoint of the basic models these four are all identical. The differences among them, as will be described shortly, are based on varying assumptions regarding economic conditions during the 1950s and assumptions regarding the size of the military force in 1960.

Although these projections to 1960 were made primarily in order to test the feasibility of the theoretical models, it is believed that the projections in themselves will have some practical application for certain types of manpower analyses. Furthermore it is hoped that the results of this study will demonstrate the advantages to be gained by extending the application of the models to more useful and at the same time more difficult data. Projection with reference only to the major occupational categories is of somewhat limited utility both because of the heterogeneous character of these broad groupings and the need for information about highly specific occupations. However, while the models now appear to be appropriate for making projections for more detailed occupational classifications, this was not apparent at the outset. To have launched a large project initially, involving hundreds of occupations, was thought not to be advisable until the feasibility of the models was established first of all on a small scale. This purpose was adequately served by the use of the classification of ten major occupational groups.

General Approach

Basically the methodology consists of a combination of cohort and component analyses. In the following paragraphs these procedures are being presented as separate forms of analysis. Actually as will be seen when the methodology is studied in detail, these are not two totally separate approaches; rather they are two avenues for viewing the process of change over time - in this case, occupational change. The approaches are intrinsically related one to another, and in their use they overlap and complement each other. For the sake of a better comprehension of the models and projections, however, and in order to make clear whatever assumptions and hypotheses are involved, we shall examine these two basic frameworks separately.

Cohort analysis. One of our basic propositions is that there is an underlying continuity within a group of individuals which carries over time; this continuity applies to a number of aspects of their lives, but here we are concerned only with their occupational composition. The occupational pattern of a specific group of men - a cohort - at any one moment of time is, in large measure, a function of their past occupational experiences. Hence their future occupational experiences to a considerable extent will be a function of their historical past and present occupational experiences.[1] For example, if we know the occupational distribution of a group of men, say aged 35 to 39 years in 1950, and their occupations in 1940 when they were 25 to 29 years old, and in 1930 when they were 15 to 19 years of age, we know one of the components needed for estimating their occupational distribution in 1960 when they will be 45 to 49 years of age. In short it is held that after tracing through the occupational history of a cohort of men, we then have a basis for projecting this history into the not too distant future with a minimum of error.

Each age cohort has its own historical pattern of occupational change which will influence its 1960 occupational distribution. The occupational composition of men aged 55 to 59 years in 1960, for example, will be different from that of men aged 45 to 49 in 1960, not only because of the differences in age, but also because the two cohorts have had different occupational histories. These differences in occupational history can be traced back to the period in which they first entered the working force. Men aged 55 to 59 years in 1960 for the most part entered the working force in the period around World War I. The cohort ten years younger in 1960 entered the working force during the boom of the later 1920s and the early part of the depression of the 1930s. Having entered at different periods, they were confronted by varying types of job opportunities and thus entered various occupations. Once having entered the working force, their subsequent careers were variously affected by prosperity and depression, by peace and war. Each of these influences affected their occupational distribution and added to the history which helped mold their subsequent occupational experiences.

Each age cohort began its working life under somewhat different conditions from every other age cohort and was differently affected by succeeding historical events. No two cohorts had identical working force experiences in the past, and therefore we assume that their future working force experiences will also be different. Hence our first line of investigation involves that of tracing through specific age cohorts historically prior to projecting these specific age cohorts to 1960.

Component analysis. Projection accuracy can also be improved by separate analysis and projection of some or all of the important components of past change. Since component analysis is so important to our model, let us review what it consists of and wherein lies its value.

Obviously it is simple to project or extrapolate totals or percentage distributions without reference to the separate components which contribute to any observed changes over time. For example, between 1930 and 1940 the numbers of nonagricultural laborers decreased by 1.4%. One assumption we could make is that if the 1950s recapitulated the economic picture of the 1930s the number of such laborers might decrease again by 1.4%. Component analysis, however, provides an estimated increase of 13.4%. This reversal in direction of change results from the fact of population growth during the 1950s; since there will be more men - particularly younger men very many of whom enter the working force as unskilled workers - the number of unskilled workers can be expected to increase.

---

1. See also below, Chapter 7, "Patterns of Working Life."

We might try to project the percentage distribution rather than the percentage change.   In 1930, 13.3 percent of the men in the working force were nonagricultural laborers; in 1940, 12.6 percent were such laborers.   In 1950, 8.7 percent were in this occupational category.   If we were to assume that the economic conditions of the 1930s were to be repeated, we should expect a proportion smaller than 8.7 to be nonagricultural laborers.   Our component analysis provides, however, an expected increase to 9.1 percent, unless we assume that large numbers of men will be drawn into the armed forces.   The fact that a larger proportion of the male working force is expected to be in this category in 1960, given the same economic conditions as the 1930s, is due to the same factors mentioned above.

Of course it is possible to project either totals or percentage distributions by specific ages.   The making of such projections is simply an adumbrated component analysis.   In short it is held that working with changes in gross figures is less reliable than working with changes in components because gross changes may cancel conflicting trends in the various components.   Any particular way in which these diverse component trends canceled each other in the past will not necessarily be recapitulated in the future.   They have to be calculated, component by component, and then summed in order to get a more probable total picture.

Changes in the gross figures are compounded of many different types of changes. One possible component of occupational change (which was not brought into our model) is the detailed occupations, the occupational sub-groupings comprising each major occupational category.   Each detailed occupation could then be viewed as a sub-component of a major grouping; projection would proceed by estimating future changes of the sub-components on the basis of past performance under specified conditions.

The model to be developed in these pages makes use of five components altogether: (1) age; (2) deaths; (3) new entries into the labor force; (4) retirements from the labor force; and (5) occupational net mobility.   Working with the major group occupational distribution of the male working force by five-year age groups, as of 1930, 1940 and 1950, intercensal patterns of occupational change for each five-year age cohort were then further sub-divided into changes occurring either through deaths, new entries, retirements or net mobility.   In this manner not only could changes be observed in the occupational distribution of an age cohort from one decade to the next, but the particular mode of change could be attributed to one of four possible components.   On the basis of this analysis, each age cohort was projected to 1960 by separately projecting each of the four components of change; then each major occupation group was projected by summing the age cohort projections.

From the point of view of component analysis, the gross changes in each occupational category are seen as the sum of the changes in each age cohort, and the changes in each age cohort as the sum of the changes in each of the four components: deaths, new entries, retirements and net mobility.   These changes in the numbers in an occupation for an age cohort from one census to the next can be expressed algebraically by the balancing equation,

(1) $O_2 = O_1 - D + NE - R \pm NM,$

where O_2 is the numbers observed in the occupation and age cohort at the end of the decade, O_1 the numbers observed at the beginning of the decade, D is intercensal deaths among the age cohort in the occupation, NE is intercensal new entries, R is intercensal retirements, and NM the net intercensal gain or loss through net mobility.

Use of the balancing equation as part of the model implies that all intercensal occupational changes in an age cohort are exhausted by the four components.   It should be observed, however, that a logically complete model would also have included working force withdrawals and reentries as components. In the case of men they are of minimal importance and have been omitted from consideration. Changes via either of these components are consequently forced over into one of the other four because of the assumption that they exhaust all possibilities of change.

Net changes. Another aspect of the general approach is the use of the net rather than gross changes for all aspects of the models except deaths. It would have been possible to build a theoretical model using gross changes; the available data, however, permitted analyses only of net changes. Hence the models were built along these lines. All of the components to be presented in the following chapters are thus net figures, representing the balance of the in-flows and out-flows, either into or out of the working force, or into or out of any specific occupation.

Use of total working force. The models devised and projections made involve the total working force - the sum of the employed plus the unemployed. No attempt was made to build into the models separate calculations for employed and unemployed for several reasons. First of all, it is impossible to make any realistic predictions regarding the exact levels of employment and unemployment in 1960; this precludes making any realistic projections of the size and occupational composition of either group at that date. The total working force, however, is much more predictable, at least with respect to its size, since it is but little affected by levels of employment.

Another reason is that from the viewpoint of manpower supply the unemployed are part of the supply. Just because the economy may not be using them at any given moment does not mean that these unemployed are not available, i.e., part of the supply. Accordingly in making any projections of manpower supply, it would be desirable to include them in addition to the employed.

Finally to build into the models procedures for handling the two groups separately would have made the models too complex within the limitations of this study. Therefore by combining the two groups into the total working force, the models became feasible, and the final end purpose of estimating supply will be satisfied.

It should be noted that men not in the working force might be considered as part of the potential supply also. However, trying to determine how many of them might be available at some future date, under what conditions they would be available, and what occupational skills they might supply are questions which seem unanswerable on the basis of available data. Only guesses can be made as to the answers. Our models, however, have to fit the available, or potentially available, data. Since there is little likelihood that the needed data about men not in the working force will become available, this group was excluded from our projected schedules of manpower supply.

Basic data utilized. Since the main purpose of this study was to develop a methodology useful in estimating the labor supply in total United States, the basic data used for testing the model were data referring to the total country. Such a limitation practically by definition means that the basic data must come from the United States decennial censuses of population; accordingly the bulk of the statistics to be presented here were obtained from this source.

It is recognized that considerable bodies of information about local labor market conditions are available. Since these statistics are delimited to local areas, it was believed that there was little point in trying to use them. A case history of New Haven, Connecticut, or San Francisco, California, no matter how complete it may be with good statistics, nevertheless is not particularly useful for testing a model which is to be applied to the entire country. Use has been made of data from the Six City

Study in Chapter 7, "Patterns of Working Life," but otherwise no use has been made of such local studies.

In theory the models could have been applied beginning with any date. Actually the 1930 census was the first one which had the minimum of reasonably usable data in accordance with the requirements of the models. If we had tried to begin at an earlier date, considerable revisions in the models would have been required for the simple reason that these earlier data are almost noncomparable with the data from the 1940 and 1950 censuses. It is recognized that the 1930 census data are not very comparable either; on the other hand, they are not as incomparable as the earlier data.

The technical problems involved in the use of these census materials as well as the details of the models are explained fully in the third part of this volume.

Basic Assumptions Used in Projecting

Continuity of the occupational structure. One basic assumption underlying the projection to 1960 is that there is an inherent stability in the occupational structure. It is recognized that occupations do change over time - new occupations appear and old ones disappear, and those which persist over the decades change so as to become unrecognizable. Every significant change in technology and the social and economic structure has repercussions on the occupational distribution of a nation.

Nevertheless within a very short period of time - say a decade - the changes which do occur are so slight as not to negate the possibility of making projections. For example, historically in the United States the automobile began to be developed around the beginning of the twentieth century. It took perhaps twenty years before any changes in the occupational structure attributable to this industry could be detected. This is not to say that highly specific individual occupations may not be materially affected in a relatively short period of time. The numbers of men in an occupation as specific as automobile chauffeur or stable hand, for example, could change greatly in a period of even less than twenty years.

On the other hand, most occupations associated with a new industry are not necessarily and entirely unique to that industry. The automobile industry, for example, employed machinists, foundrymen and other types of occupations which had been in existence before the automobile industry. The effect of the growth of the automobile industry on some of these occupations was to increase their numbers and perhaps to change the specific duties of the individuals involved, to some extent. However, in light of the total occupational structure of the country, it is contended that these occupational changes occasioned by the growth of the automobile industry were relatively minor in the short run.

In the long run of course, over a period of several decades, these small changes accumulate until they noticeably modify the occupational structure. This is what makes projections several decades into the future of considerably less value than are projections into the near future.

It is possible that the present development in nuclear physics and atomic energy may ultimately result in occupational changes as great as were those occasioned by the first Industrial Revolution in the eighteenth century. It is believed, however, that by 1960 these changes will have been so slight, except in a few very highly specific occupations intimately associated with the atomic energy program, that the 1960 census will show almost no reflection of these occupational changes. We should remember that most of the people engaged in this program are in occupations which were already in existence and have been in existence for some time - carpenters and cement workers, office workers, machinists, chemists, and a whole host of familiar occupations.

<u>Economic and labor market conditions.</u> The second basic assumption taken into consideration is that the occupations in which men find themselves at any given moment are in part a reflection of the business cycle at that time. The phase of the business cycle sets the framework for the labor demand schedules of the economy. The demand for labor then interacts with the supply of labor to form the specific occupational distribution observed at any given time. The phrase "given time" or "given moment" is used here to include more than just a brief period of time, but rather an extended period covering an entire phase of the business cycle. It is not anticipated that the occupational structure will change markedly in the space of a few months or even a year in response to changes in the business cycle. However, if a phase of the business cycle persists for some time, as was the case of the depression years of the 1930s, or the prosperity years of the 1940s, then the demand schedules interacting with the supply schedules can bring about noticeable changes in the occupational structure.

Furthermore it should be emphasized that such cyclical variations in the occupational structure are superimposed upon any long-time trends which may be occurring due to basic technological, social and economic changes. The continuity of the occupational structure previously referred to can be considered as the trend line depicting the direction of the long-time changes which are occurring. Superimposed upon these long-time changes are the short-run variations related to the changes in the business cycle.

This assumption regarding the relationship of the business cycle to the occupational structure includes another assumption, namely, that men can move about occupationally within certain prescribed limits from one job to another job. Thus although there is an underlying continuity to an individual's occupational history, this continuity is only approximate. Only in a very rigid society such as one having slaves or serfs might the occupation of a person remain constant throughout his life. In a dynamic society certain changes are possible. The types of changes possible on the one hand are set by the personal characteristics of the individual - his education, abilities, etc. - and on the other hand by the opportunities presented by the economy, i.e., the labor market or demand conditions as of a given time.

For the purpose of the models presented here, it was neither feasible nor entirely pertinent that all of the labor market conditions which could affect the demand side be examined and dissected. Rather use was made of the very diverse experiences of the decades of the 1930s and 1940s to set approximately outer limits on the demand schedules.

The 1930s were a period of great depression and little expansion of the economy. Unemployment was high, and there was comparatively little opportunity for individuals to make marked shifts in their occupational position. For example, farmers were prevented from leaving their farms because of the lack of nonagricultural jobs; persons desiring to establish themselves in businesses were prevented by the lack of capital and the apparent lack of business opportunities; operatives failed to rise to craftsmen's jobs if for no other reason than that the economy already had more craftsmen than it could use. In short this decade might be characterized very briefly as a decade of stagnation. Men tended to remain occupationally where they were at the beginning of the decade, and there was little opportunity for them to move elsewhere.[2]

To this was added the impetus to create more job vacancies for younger people by retiring more older persons from the working force. This was one of the factors

---

2. See also Charles A. Meyer, <u>Mobility and Economic Opportunity</u>, Chapter 4, "Labor Mobility in Two Communities."

contributing to the acceptance of the Federal old age and survivors' insurance program which was adopted during this decade.

Simultaneously youngsters remained in school rather than entering the working force. Between 1930 and 1940, for example, enrollment in secondary schools increased from 4,800,000 to 7,100,000, an increase of 2,300,000. During this decade, however, the number of youths of high school age remained about the same; there were approximately twelve million youths (of both sexes) at the beginning and end of the decade.

During the 1940s by contrast the demand side for labor was quite different. Unemployment fell to all-time lows, and there were work opportunities for almost everyone who desired them. Teen-agers could and did enter the working force in greater numbers, and older people, many of whom were eligible to retire, remained in the working force. Opportunities to shift from job to job and from occupation to occupation were available to a much greater extent than during the 1930s. In almost all respects the prosperous economic conditions of the 1940s provided a pattern of labor demand which was about as completely different from that of the 1930s as can be expected.

The theoretical models which we constructed are independent of such labor market conditions. They can be applied to either periods of depression or periods of prosperity with equal facility; however, in making the projections to 1960, whatever diverse economic conditions we want to assume can be projected by simply introducing those conditions into the calculations. What we did was to assume for one set of projections that the economic and labor market conditions of the 1930s would prevail during the 1950s and for the second set of projections that the sum totality of the economic conditions of the 1940s would prevail.

Introduction

As was described previously, the main purpose for making arithmetic projections was to test the feasibility of the models when applied to the kinds of data actually available. In doing so, complete projections to 1960 resulted. It is believed furthermore that such projections would have substantive as well as methodological interest. They present a pre-view of what the occupational structure for men in the United States in 1960 may be and as such can have value in analyses of future manpower supply schedules.

In this section therefore will be presented the total expected occupational distribution in 1960, and the changes in numbers of persons in each major occupation group, for the period 1930 to 1960. The components of these changes - the numbers of new entries into each occupation for each decade, the net mobility among occupations, retirements and deaths, all these components for individual age cohorts - will be presented and analyzed separately in Part II.

Four sets of projections are presented here, labelled for convenience' sake: A, B, A' and B'. Let us but briefly describe them here; the complete details of their computations are presented in Part III.

The two A series are based on the assumption that labor market conditions in the 1950s will be similar to those of the 1930s. This assumption was built into the projections by assuming the same patterns as were observed in the 1930s of: new entries by age and occupation; net mobility among the various occupations for each five-year age cohort; and retirements by age and occupation. Mortality conditions, however, were taken as those assumed to be appropriate to the 1950s. These patterns were then applied to the 1950 civilian male working force by age and occupation, as reported in the 1950 United States Decennial Census.

The two B series are based on the assumption that in the 1950s economic and labor market conditions will be similar to those of the 1940s. Thus the patterns of new entries, mobility and retirements were those observed in the 1940s. The mortality conditions assumed for this series are identical to those used for the A series.

The patterns of new entries, mobility and retirement as observed in the 1930s and 1940s were all computed in accordance with the models designed as part of this study. Hence exactly the same procedures were applied to the basic census data covering these two decades in order to obtain what we are here referring to as the "observed patterns." These two sets of observed patterns were then applied to the 1950 male working force, by five-year age cohorts and major occupation groups as reported in the 1950 United States census, in exactly the same way. As a result the two sets of projections are methodologically completely comparable. They differ only to the extent that the economic conditions of the two decades prior to the 1950s are different.

Since the economic and related demand schedules for labor were so different in these two decades, it is believed that these two projections, A and B, may represent the two most extreme occupational distributions which are likely to occur in the 1950s. It is not anticipated that any possible depression period will be worse than that of the 1930s, nor does it seem possible that any period of prosperity is likely to have more "full employment" than was observed in the 1940s. In short it is thought that a continuation of peacetime conditions to 1960 will result in an occupational distribution for men in the civilian working force in that year within the extremes of the A and B series as presented here.

In making projections into the future, all likely considerations regarding developments should be taken into account insofar as possible. One such consideration that is very important involves conditions of war or peace and the size of the armed forces as of 1960. These are intangibles beyond the powers of our models to encompass. Fortunately from all viewpoints, including that of the calculations made for this study, the pivotal dates for which the basic data were obtained - namely, 1930, 1940 and 1950 - were periods of peace and ones in which the size of the United States armed forces was relatively small. The census of 1940 preceded the entry of the United States into the Second World War by almost two years, and even the 1950 census preceded the Korean outbreak by some three months. Whether we shall have peace or war in the 1950s and what the size of the United States armed forces will be in 1960, the models do not tell us. Hence in the unfortunate event of catastrophic conditions in 1960 the occupational composition of the civilian male working force in that year (assuming a census is even taken) is left to the imagination.

It is of course possible to build into the projections any assumptions that it is desired to make regarding the size and age composition of the armed forces in 1960. In constructing the A and B projections, allowance was made for only a small number of men in the armed forces. The exact procedures whereby such allowances were made are rather complicated and are described in Chapter 15. Very briefly it can be said that for ages 30 and over in 1960 the military levels were assumed to be about of the same magnitude as in 1950 for the comparable age groups. For the ages under 30 in 1960 it was assumed that the military levels would be of about the same size as were observed in 1950 for members of the armed forces stationed outside Continental United States.

In addition, another set of projections was made which assumed military levels as of 1950, prior to the Korean outbreak. This second series assumes that there will be about 700,000 more men in the military than were assumed in the first series. Otherwise the A' projection is exactly the same as the A projection because it takes into consideration the economic conditions of the 1930s; also the B' projection is the same as the B projection because it takes into consideration the economic conditions of the 1940s.

Projected Numbers of Workers

The total male population (between the ages of 15 and 74 years) increased from 42.9 millions in 1930 to 48.1 in 1940, 52.5 in 1950, and is expected to number some 57.3 millions in 1960. This is a growth of about 14.4 millions of men distributed by decades as follows:

1930 to 1940	5.2 millions increase
1940 to 1950	4.4 millions increase
1950 to 1960	4.8 millions increase

These changes in the numbers of men are a composite of changes in past fertility, volume of foreign migration, and decreases in mortality. The factors associated with these population changes are beyond the scope of this investigation, however, and will not be presented here.

The numbers of civilian men in the working force increased during this period from 37.3 million in 1930 to 39.0 in 1940 to 42.3 in 1950. In 1960 it is estimated that the total numbers will range from a minimum of 45.0 million to a maximum of 46.8 million, depending on future conditions (Table 1). The minimum size working force is expected if the economic conditions of the 1950s should be similar to those of the 1930s and if the size of the armed forces should be about the same as it was in April,

MALE WORKING FORCE (AGED 15-74 YEARS) BY OCCUPATION, 1930, 1940, 1950 AND 1960
(Numbers in Thousands)

| Occupation | 1930 | 1940 | 1950 | 1960 Projections | | | |
| | | | | Based on 1930's experience | | Based on 1940's experience | |
				A	A'	B	B'
Professional, technical and kindred workers	1709.4	2242.7	3076.0	3613.1	3586.6	3881.9	3844.4
Farmers and farm managers	5627.0	5091.7	4222.2	4293.2	4251.3	3775.9	3740.3
Managers, officials and proprietors, except farm	3570.5	3411.0	4373.1	4229.7	4211.6	5211.9	5188.6
Clerical and kindred workers	2088.9	2285.8	2749.7	2801.6	2753.0	3070.8	3012.3
Sales workers	2130.6	2332.7	2673.4	2910.7	2859.3	3030.7	2972.2
Craftsmen, foremen and kindred workers	6128.3	5963.4	8074.3	7940.6	7878.1	9977.5	9884.4
Operatives and kindred workers	5795.8	7165.6	8737.1	9865.2	9709.7	9923.1	9744.8
Service workers	1791.8	2389.0	2614.2	3154.3	3111.7	2758.1	2717.3
Farm laborers and foremen	3519.9	3233.0	2063.8	2715.7	2575.6	1988.2	1895.5
Laborers except farm and mine	4975.3	4903.3	3681.4	4174.5	4061.8	3150.4	3068.8
All occupations	37337.5	39018.2	42265.2	45698.6	44998.7	46768.5	46068.6
Population 15 to 74	42913.4	48096.9	52478.4	57321.8	57321.8	57321.8	57321.8
Percent in working force	87.0	81.1	80.5	80.0	78.5	81.6	80.0

TABLE 2

PERCENTAGE DISTRIBUTION OF MALE WORKING FORCE BY OCCUPATION, 1930, 1940, 1950 AND 1960

| Occupation | 1930 | 1940 | 1950 | 1960 Projections | | | |
| | | | | Based on 1930's experience | | Based on 1940's experience | |
				A	A'	B	B'
Professional, technical and kindred workers	4.6	5.7	7.3	7.9	8.0	8.3	8.3
Farmers and farm managers	15.1	13.0	10.0	9.4	9.4	8.1	8.1
Managers, officials and proprietors, except farm	9.6	8.7	10.3	9.3	9.4	11.1	11.3
Clerical and kindred workers	5.6	5.9	6.5	6.1	6.1	6.6	6.5
Sales workers	5.7	6.0	6.3	6.4	6.4	6.5	6.5
Craftsmen, foremen and kindred workers	16.4	15.3	19.1	17.4	17.5	21.3	21.5
Operatives and kindred workers	15.5	18.4	20.7	21.6	21.6	21.2	21.2
Service workers	4.8	6.1	6.2	6.9	6.9	5.9	5.9
Farm laborers and foremen	9.4	8.3	4.9	5.9	5.7	4.3	4.1
Laborers except farm and mine	13.3	12.6	8.7	9.1	9.0	6.7	6.7
All occupations	100.0	100.0	100.0	100.0	100.0	100.0	100.0

Source: Based on data shown in Table 1.

1950. The maximum number of men in the working force is estimated by assuming that economic conditions will be similar to those of the 1940s and that the size of the armed forces will be approximately that of the period preceding the Second World War.[1]

The proportions of all men (between the ages of 15 and 74) who were, or are projected to be, in the civilian working force thus are:

1930	87.0 percent
1940	81.1 percent
1950	80.5 percent
1960	

Projection B (maximum)	81.6 percent
Projection B'	80.4 percent
Projection A	79.7 percent
Projection A' (minimum)	78.5 percent

By varying the assumptions regarding the size of the military forces in 1960, other estimates of the size of the civilian working force can be had. It is believed that under normal peacetime conditions in which the United States is not mobilized for military purposes there would not be fewer than 45.7 millions (projection A) and not more than 46.8 millions (projection B) of men in the civilian working force.

To these numbers of course can be added a very small number of boys aged 14 and men aged 75 and over who will be in the working force. In 1950 there were about 400,000 persons in these two extreme age groups who were in the working force, or perhaps 1 percent of the total male working force. If it is desired to include in the 1960 projections estimates for these two extreme age groups the 1960 totals (shown in Table 1) can be increased by about 1 percent.

Projected Occupational Distribution

The projected occupational distributions for 1960 show considerable divergence for some groups as among the four series. It is clear that the two groups "craftsmen, foremen, and kindred workers" and "operatives and kindred workers" will continue to be the two largest groups in 1960, just as they were in 1940 and 1950 (Table 2). The proportion who may be in the craftsmen category varies from a low of 17.4 percent (A' projection) to a high of 21.5 percent (B' projection). Operatives are expected to vary only from between 21.2 percent (B and B' projections) and 21.6 percent (A and A' projections).

---

1. It should be noted that these working force projections are not entirely comparable with other projections which have been made; see for example, "A Projected Growth of the Labor Force in the United States Under Conditions of High Employment: 1950 to 1975," U. S. Bureau of the Census, Series P-50, No. 42, December 10, 1952. The sources of incomparability between the census estimates and ours are: (a) census includes military whereas we do not; (b) the 1950 working force levels which census uses as a base point provide a male working force which is 4.2 millions greater than the one we used. We began with the civilian working force data by age as presented in the 1950 census. The census in adjusting their data increased the size by the above amount. Our B' projection (full employment with military levels about equal to pre-Korea) is the projection most nearly comparable to the census projections. Our estimate was 46.1 millions. If to this is added the 4.2 million discrepancy between the census and our 1950 totals, we arrive at an estimated working force in 1960 of 50.3 millions. This latter is exactly the size as projected in the census release.

Farm owners will decrease proportionally according to all four projections. In 1950, 10 percent of the men were "farmers and farm managers." This may fall to only 9.4 percent (A projection) or as low as 8.1 percent (B and B' projections). "Farm laborers and foremen" will constitute but a small proportion of the total civilian male working force. In 1950 they constituted 4.9 percent. The 1960 projections show them ranging from 4.1 percent to 5.9 percent.

The major divergencies among the 1960 projections are clearly attributable to possible variations in economic conditions during the 1950s. Only minor variations result from the assumptions regarding the size of the military establishment. For example, under a repetition of the conditions of the 1930s the number of "professional, technical and related workers" are expected to increase by about 17 percent over 1950. If the economic conditions of the 1940s are repeated, then this group will increase in size by about 26 percent over 1950. In the event that many men are mobilized into the military, the percentage increases will be smaller in both instances (Table 3).

Repetition of the 1930s' conditions will result in an increase of 32 percent among agricultural workers whereas repetition of the 1940s' labor market situation will result in a decrease of about 4 percent. With respect to this occupational group, withdrawal into the military will decrease the numbers considerably. This results from the fact that agricultural laborers are primarily younger men of military age so that many more of them than of farm owners, for example, would be inducted.

Variations attributable to economic conditions. These can be noted by comparing the percentage change expected between 1950 and the A projection with that expected from the B projection. In the case of "laborers, except farm and mine," for example, the A projection provides an increase of 13.4 percent whereas the B projection provides a decrease of 14.4 percent. Algebraic addition of these two changes shows they diverge by 27.8 percentage points (Table 3). Clearly under depression conditions there would be many more laborers than under conditions of full employment.

The difference between the A and B projections can be summarized as follows. Depression conditions would lead to:

a. Greatly increased numbers of men as:

Farm laborers and foremen
Laborers, except farm and mine

b. Somewhat smaller increases in the numbers in:

Service workers
Farmers and farm managers

There is expected to be very little difference as between depression and prosperity with respect to the numbers of men engaged as:

Operatives and kindred workers
Sales workers

Prosperous conditions and a booming economy should lead to:

a. Big increase in the numbers of men in the groups:

Managers, officials and proprietors, except farm
Craftsmen, foremen and kindred workers

  b. Somewhat smaller increases in the numbers in:

       Professional, technical and kindred workers
       Clerical and kindred workers

     This pattern of differences between depression and prosperity conditions seems
in accordance with what might be expected. During depression men in agriculture remain
there since they have difficulties in obtaining nonagricultural work. Many of them become part of the pool of hidden unemployment, whether they are sons who are unpaid
family farm laborers or "farm owners" - including, as this category does, renters and
sharecroppers as well as men who actually own their farms.

     Men are dammed up in the category of nonagricultural laborers also. There are
few opportunities for them to advance even to the level of operatives, so they remain
laborers whether employed or unemployed.

     During prosperous times on the other hand many men work their way from non-
agricultural laborer to operative and from operative to craftsman. In this process
the size of the operative group remains more nearly constant while the group of laborers decreases significantly and the group of craftsmen increases greatly in size.

     During booming times also, business opportunities being much better, there is
a substantial increase in the numbers of managers, officials and proprietors of nonagricultural enterprises. Many of these men come from the ranks of clerical and sales
people; others come from the ranks of craftsmen and foremen who become managers and
officials in the establishments in which employed. More men enter the professions
also, if for no other reason than that during prosperity they can afford to study at
colleges and universities and thus qualify for professional jobs.[2]

     The total male working force in 1960 is expected to be a little larger under
prosperous conditions. An increase of 10.7 percent is projected under these conditions
whereas under depression conditions it is anticipated that it would increase by only
8.1 percent, or 2.6 percentage points fewer. This too seems reasonable since under
conditions of full employment more youths enter the labor force and fewer older men
retire.[3] The difference is not very great, however, and may amount to only about 1.1
millions of men.

     Variations attributable to the size of the military forces. These can be
noted by examining the percentage changes between 1950 and the A projection, and that
with the A' projection (or those obtained from the B and B' projections). These variations are much smaller than those noted as resulting from differential economic conditions; only if it were assumed that the military forces were very large might there be
larger differences in the male civilian occupational structure which can be attributed
to the military.

     The main effect of withdrawals into the military is upon the younger age
groups. Hence those occupations in which younger men predominate are the ones most
likely to be affected by the size of the military establishment. This can be seen by
comparing the median ages of the occupations with the projected effects of entries into
the military, as follows:

---

2 See Chapter 7, "Patterns of Working Life."

3. For a discussion of the relationship between unemployment and retirement, see
Chapter 6, "Retirements."

Occupations above average age in 1950	Effects of entries into military[4]
Managers, officials and proprietors, except farm	0.4
Farmers and farm managers	1.0
Craftsmen, foremen and kindred workers	0.7
Professional, technical and kindred workers	0.8
Service workers	1.7
Average	0.9

Occupations below average age in 1950	
Sales workers	1.9
Operatives and kindred workers	1.8
Farm laborers and foremen	6.8
Laborers except farm and mine	3.1
Clerical and kindred workers	1.8
Average	3.1
All occupations	1.6

Of course if the size of the military were greatly expanded in 1960, as was the situation during the Second World War, the resulting effects upon the occupational composition of the civilian male population would be much more drastic than that shown here. The production needed to maintain such a military establishment would have to be carried out, but much of such production can be done by women workers. Hence it is conceivable that the occupational composition of the total working force might be altered much less than that of the men workers under such conditions.

Changes in age composition

The civilian male working force has aged somewhat since 1930. In that year the median age of the total working force was 37.2 years. This increased to 37.9 years in 1940 and 39.2 years in 1950; over the twenty-year period the working force became, on the average, two years older.

This trend toward increasing average age will continue into 1960. It is expected that the working force at that date may be about one year older, on the average, than it was in 1950. The expected median ages for the four projections are as follows:

Projection	Median age
A	40.0 years
B	40.1 years
A'	40.3 years
B'	40.4 years

Under conditions of prosperity it is expected that more older men will remain in the working force instead of retiring, and therefore the median age will be somewhat higher than if depression conditions prevail.

In the event of large-scale military mobilization the median age will be somewhat higher also, because large numbers of the younger men will have been withdrawn from civilian life.

---

4. Difference between the A and A' projections, index numbers showing percentage change since 1950 (see Table 3).

TABLE 3

INDEX NUMBERS OF CHANGES IN SIZE OF MALE WORKING FORCE BY OCCUPATION, 1930, 1940, 1950 AND 1960

1930 = 100

	1930	1940	1950	1960 A'	1960 A	1960 B	1960 B'
Professional, technical and kindred workers	100.0	131.2	179.9	209.8	211.4	227.1	224.9
Farmers and farm managers	100.0	90.5	75.0	75.6	76.3	67.1	66.5
Managers, officials and proprietors, except farm	100.0	95.5	122.5	118.0	118.5	146.0	145.3
Clerical and kindred workers	100.0	109.4	131.6	131.8	134.1	147.0	144.2
Sales workers	100.0	109.5	125.5	134.2	136.6	142.2	139.5
Craftsmen, foremen and kindred workers	100.0	97.3	131.8	128.6	129.6	162.8	161.3
Operatives and kindred workers	100.0	123.6	150.7	167.5	170.2	171.2	168.1
Service workers	100.0	133.3	145.9	173.7	176.0	153.9	151.7
Farm laborers and foremen	100.0	91.8	58.6	73.2	77.2	56.6	53.9
Laborers except farm and mine	100.0	98.6	74.0	81.6	83.9	63.3	61.7
All occupations	100.0	104.5	113.2	120.5	122.4	125.3	123.4

1950 = 100

	1930	1940	1950	1960 A'	1960 A	1960 B	1960 B'	Differences A-A'	Differences B-A	Differences B-B'
Professional, technical and kindred workers	55.6	73.0	100.0	116.7	117.5	126.3	125.1	0.8	8.8	1.2
Farmers and farm managers	133.3	120.6	100.0	100.7	101.7	89.4	88.6	1.0	12.3	0.8
Managers, officials and proprietors, except farm	81.6	78.0	100.0	96.3	96.7	119.2	118.6	0.4	22.5	0.6
Clerical and kindred workers	76.0	83.1	100.0	100.1	101.9	111.7	109.6	1.8	9.8	2.1
Sales workers	79.7	87.3	100.0	107.0	108.9	113.4	111.2	1.9	4.5	2.2
Craftsmen, foremen and kindred workers	75.9	73.9	100.0	97.6	98.3	123.6	122.4	0.7	25.3	1.2
Operatives and kindred workers	66.3	82.0	100.0	111.1	112.9	113.6	111.5	1.8	0.7	2.1
Service workers	68.5	91.4	100.0	119.0	120.7	105.6	103.9	1.7	-15.1	1.7
Farm laborers and foremen	170.6	156.7	100.0	124.8	131.6	96.3	91.8	6.8	-35.3	4.5
Laborers except farm and mine	135.1	133.2	100.0	110.3	113.4	85.6	83.4	3.1	-27.8	2.2
All occupations	88.3	92.3	100.0	106.5	108.1	110.7	109.0	1.6	2.6	1.7

Source: Based on data shown in Table 1.

The changes to be expected in individual occupation groups are quite variable, however. The maximum variation expected is for the service occupations; under prosperity conditions (projection B) the median age is expected to be 45.0 years, whereas under depression conditions (projection A) an average of 42.8 years is expected, or a difference of 2.2 years (Table 4).

With respect to the following occupation groups the A and B projections provide about identical median ages:

Farmers and farm managers
Managers, officials and proprietors, except farm
Operatives and kindred workers

The factors other than the size of the military forces which are relevant in affecting median age are: (a) the rates of new entries for the various occupations which help to determine the numbers of younger men, and (b) the rates of retirements which help determine the numbers of older men. In addition, variations in the rates of mobility among the occupation groups help determine whether younger men remain dammed up in certain occupations or move on to others. These separate considerations will be examined in detail in Part II. The numbers of men by age who were in each occupation in 1930, 1940 and 1950 and the numbers expected in 1960 under the various assumptions are shown in Appendix Table 1.

TABLE 4
MEDIAN AGE OF MALE WORKING FORCE BY OCCUPATION, 1950 AND 1960

	1950	1960 A	1960 B	B-A
Professional, technical and kindred workers	38.6	41.6	40.2	-1.4
Farmers and farm managers	45.4	43.9	44.3	0.4
Managers, officials and proprietors, except farm	44.5	46.3	46.0	-0.3
Clerical and kindred workers	35.9	39.2	37.4	-1.8
Sales workers	36.8	37.5	36.7	-0.8
Craftsmen, foremen and kindred workers	40.6	43.3	41.6	-1.7
Operatives and kindred workers	35.8	37.6	37.3	-0.3
Service workers	43.7	42.8	45.0	2.2
Farm laborers and foremen	26.8	23.0	22.0	-1.0
Laborers except farm and mine	36.8	32.8	34.1	1.3
All occupations	39.2	40.0	40.1	0.1

TABLE 5
COMPONENTS OF CHANGE IN THE MALE WORKING FORCE
(AGED 4-74 YEARS AS OF THE BEGINNING OF THE DECADE)
1930-40, 1940-50 AND 1950-60
(Numbers in Thousands)

	1930 to 1940	1940 to 1950	1950 to 1960 A	A'	B	B*
Number at beginning of decade	37,448.3	39,083.9	42,396.7	42,396.7	42,396.7	42,396
Changes during decade						
New entries	9,737.6	9,944.3	10,068.7	9,368.8	10,411.0	9,711
Deaths	5,449.5	4,021.4	4,333.3	4,333.3	4,333.3	4,333
Retirements	2,652.5	2,610.1	3,535.3	3,535.3	2,867.9	2,867
Additional entries*	-	-	1,101.8	1,101.8	1,162.1	1,162
Sum of net changes	1,635.6	3,312.8	3,301.9	2,602.0	4,371.9	3,672
Number at end of decade	39,083.9	42,396.7	45,698.6	44,998.7	46,768.6	46,068

* Estimated number of men who were in the armed forces or who were veterans not in the civilia
working force in 1950, but who can be expected to have entered the civilian working force by
1960. See Chapter 15 for further information.

CHAPTER 3
SUMMARY OF COMPONENTS OF CHANGE

The differential action of those forces which brought men into the working
force versus those forces which took men out resulted in changes in the size of the
working force in past decades as it will in expected changes in the 1950s. We are not
trying to measure these forces; we know only how many men entered the working force in
the previous decades, i.e., new entries; and how many left, i.e., deaths and retirements. When studying individual occupations, we also know the net mobility and hence
know whether specific occupations gained or lost by such movement; the whole working
force obviously is unaffected by mobility among the occupations. In this Part II we
intend to investigate in some detail each of these components separately to ascertain
the role it has played in the past and to estimate its probable importance in the future. In addition, however, these components are interrelated and influence each other;
accordingly, they must also be examined simultaneously to note both how they interre-
late and what their relative magnitudes are. In Chapter 3 we are doing exactly this
- summarizing the various components simultaneously so that their respective magnitudes
can be approximated, both historically and in the near future.

The Entire Working Force

Changes in the decade 1930 to 1940. During this decade there were an estimated 9.7 millions of new entries. During the same period, however, about 5.5 millions
of men who had been in the civilian working force at the beginning of the decade died,
and another 2.6 millions retired and survived to the end of the decade. Thus the entire working force increased by some 1.6 millions (Table 5).

In comparison with the number in the working force at the beginning of the
decade - about 37.5 millions - the new entries constituted about 26 percent, and deaths
and retirements constituted some 21.6 percent. Hence the total civilian working force
grew by about 4.4 percent. In 1940 there were about 39.1 millions of men in the working force.

The events of this decade might be recapitulated by saying that there were almost twice as many new entries as deaths and almost twice as many deaths as retirements.
Furthermore there were very few men in the armed forces at either the beginning or end
of this period; the dynamics of the civilian male working force were largely uncompli-
cated by shifts between civilian and military status. Another factor which led to the
simplification of the analysis of this decade is the fact that there was virtually no
foreign migration; there were no measurable changes in the working force which could
be attributed to immigration or emigration.

Changes in the decade 1940 to 1950. There were an estimated 9.9 millions of
new entries during this decade. On the other hand, about 4.0 million men who had been
in the working force at the beginning of the decade subsequently died, and another 2.6
million retired. Thus the entire civilian working force increased by some 3.3 millions.

At the beginning of the decade there were about 39.1 millions of men in the
working force. Of this number the new entries constituted some 25.4 percent and deaths
and retirements about 16.9 percent. Hence the working force grew by about 8.5 percent
and numbered some 42.4 millions of men at the end of the decade, i.e., as of April,
1950.

In brief it appears that there were about two and one-half times as many new
entries as deaths and about one and one-half times as many deaths as retirements.
Analysis of the growth of the civilian working force during the period 1940 to 1950
is somewhat complicated by the fact that there were so many more men in the armed
forces in 1950 than there were in 1940. There were perhaps a million more men in the
armed forces in 1950 than there had been in 1940. Furthermore these men were concentrated largely among the younger ages and therefore largely affect the numbers of new
entries. Perhaps there would have been an additional three quarters of a million,
more or less, new entries during this period if there had been no increase in the size
of the military establishment.

Foreign immigration during this decade continued to be small, particularly
in comparison with the decades prior to 1930. The United States male civilian working
force may have been increased by perhaps some 300,000 men due to foreign immigration
during this decade,[1] a figure well under 1 percent of the number in the working force
at the beginning of the period.

Comparison of the changes in the two decades. Between 1930 and 1940 the
number of men in the working force increased by about 1.6 millions and during the following decade by about 3.3 millions. In short during the period 1940 to 1950 the working force grew by about 1.7 millions of men more than it had in the preceding decade.
What accounted for this increased growth? Far and away the most important factor was
the decrease in the death rate which resulted in a greatly decreased number of deaths.
There were 1.5 million fewer deaths in the 1940s than there were in the 1930s – 4.0
millions as compared with 5.5 millions.

The number of new entries increased but very little in the 1940s as compared
with the preceding decade – 9.9 millions as compared with 9.7, or an increase of .2
millions. Hence the large decrease in the death rate plus the small increase in the
number of new entries accounted for the entire increase in growth during the 1940s as
compared with the 1930s. During the 1940s the male working force grew more than it
did during the 1930s because many fewer men died, and a small number of additional
boys entered the working force. The numbers of retirements in the two decades were
virtually identical.

As mentioned previously, if the size of the military establishment had not
increased between 1940 and 1950, perhaps there would have been an additional .7 or .8
millions of new entries into the civilian working force. This "inherent" growth in
the number of new entries is largely a function of the relatively high birth rates and
large-scale foreign immigration of the 1920s. During the 1920s the birth rate was
well over 25 per 1000 population, after which it fell sharply and did not regain this
level until after the Second World War. During this decade also some 4 million immigrants arrived. There were comparatively few young children among these immigrants,
children who would enter the working force during the 1940s. On the other hand, these
immigrants were in part responsible for the large numbers of births during the 1920s
and thus indirectly contributed to the growth of the working force in the 1940s.

With reference to retirements it is clear that since the total numbers in the
two decades were almost exactly the same, that the retirement rate in the 1940s must
have been somewhat lower than in the 1930s since the total working force was both
larger and older in 1940 than in 1930.[2] As will be shown in Chapter 6, this was the

---

1. See Chapter 10 for further details.

2. See Tables 1 and 4.

case. These differences in rates of retirement reflect the differences in economic conditions between these two decades to a large extent. We might compare retirements with new entries by saying that in the short run the volume of retirements tends to be influenced by labor market and economic conditions, whereas the volume of new entries tends to be influenced by the volume of military requirements. The volume of retirements and new entries in the long run of course are also influenced by population changes.

Possible changes in the decade 1950 to 1960. It is estimated that the increase in the size of the civilian male working force between 1950 and 1960 will vary from between 2.6 and 4.4 millions, depending on labor market and economic conditions during the 1950s and the size of the military establishment in 1960. The smallest projected increase will occur if the economic conditions of the 1930s are repeated and there are many men in the armed forces (projection A' in Table 5) and the largest if the economic conditions of the 1940s are repeated and there are few men in the armed forces (projection B). These projections suggest that the increment in the size of the civilian working force during the 1950s will be of about the same magnitude as during the previous decade. If the economic conditions of the 1930s are recapitulated and there are few men in the armed forces, or if the economic conditions of the 1940s are repeated and there are many men in the armed forces in 1960 (projections A and B' respectively), then the working force will increase by some 3.3 to 3.7 millions. During the 1940s the working force increased by 3.3 millions. The assumption of prosperity and but little military (projection B) supplies a larger projected increase, of about 4.4 millions; as of 1954 this seems to be an unlikely event. The assumption of deep depression with or without a large military establishment, also seems to be less likely − at least from the perspective of 1954. We conclude then that perhaps the B' projection of 3.7 millions increase seems the most possible.

The number of deaths during the 1950s will be substantially the same as in the 1940s. It is estimated that there will be about 4.3 millions of deaths, or only .3 million more than in the 1940s. This number of deaths applies to all four projections. The small increase in the number of deaths will result primarily from the aging of the working force. As noted previously, the median age of the working force will increase by about one year between 1950 and 1960 (see Table 4). Despite the expected decrease in the age specific death rates, then the total number of deaths will increase. Of course the size of the working force in 1950 was larger than in 1940 so that some increase in the number of deaths would have occurred even if the age specific death rates and age composition had remained unchanged.

The projected number of retirements is largely a function of economic conditions. If jobs are as plentiful as during the 1940s, then it is projected that but 2.9 millions will retire (the B projections). If jobs are scarce, then an estimated 3.5 millions may retire both voluntarily and involuntarily (the A projections). In comparison with the decades before 1950 it seems certain that the number of retirements in the 1950s will be larger than 2.6 millions in the two previous decades. The expected increase will result from the aging of the working force, previously mentioned, together with the growth of the working force. Of course if the age specific retirement rates should change greatly during the 1950s, the absolute number of retirements would change also. It seems to us improbable, however, that the retirement rates will change sufficiently by 1960 so as to produce a number of retirements outside the range shown here (Table 5).

Analysis of the projections of numbers of new entries is a more complex problem. One generalization which seems certain is that the number of new entries is not likely to be very much greater, if at all, than it was during the 1940s. This is simply because there will be a smaller number of boys in the population than there

was in 1940.   There were about 11 million youths age 10 to 19 years in 1950 as compared
with about 12 million in 1940.

This smaller number in 1950 is a direct result of the low birth rates of the
1930s.   During the late 1930s and early 1940s the number of births, and the birth rate,
increased over the levels of the early 1930s.[3]   This increase in past fertility, however, was not enough to increase the numbers of boys reaching their teens in the 1950s,
i.e., becoming of working force age.   The big increase in fertility came after the
Second World War; these boys will begin to enter the working force in the 1960s so
that during this decade there should be many more new entries than are projected for
the decade of the 1950s.

The maximum number of new entries, 10.4 millions, is projected under conditions of economic prosperity and a small military establishment.   As of 1954 it seems
improbable that but few young men will be in the armed forces, and hence the B' projection seems more plausible.   This provides a number of 9.7 million new entries as compared with 9.9 millions during the 1940s.   In the event of depression conditions during
the 1950s (similar to those of the 1930s) the number of new entries will be even
smaller.

For the purposes of simplifying the analysis, we may hypothesize that the B'
projection – economic conditions as of the 1940s and the same number in the armed forces
as of 1950 – is the most likely.   The changes shown by this projection can be summarized as follows: 9.7 million new entries, minus 4.3 million deaths and minus 2.9 million retirements, which changes provide a net increase of 2.5 million men in the working force.

It is expected, however, that the civilian working force will grow through
the entry, or re-entry, of men who in 1950 were members of the armed forces or veterans
who had not yet returned to the civilian working force.   It is estimated that some 1.2
millions of such men who were not in the civilian working force in 1950 will have entered by 1960.   Adding these 1.2 millions to the previously mentioned increase of 2.5
millions provides a projected total increase of some 3.7 millions.

Speculation is possible about the projection of these changes beyond 1960.
Of course our models could have been carried through 1970, but such arithmetic calculations were not made.   Instead we can reason about as follows.   The numbers of deaths
and retirements during the 1960s should approximate that of the 1950s, whichever set
of economic conditions is assumed for comparative analysis.   The number of men who will
shift between military and civilian is indefinite of course since it will depend on the
number who will be in the military in 1960.   The number of new entries during the 1960s,
however, may be about one million greater than in the 1950s due to the expected increase in the number of boys becoming of working force age.   This increase will be the
direct result of the large increase in fertility following the Second World War.   In
summary then if our four projections had been made to 1970, all of them should have
shown a larger increase in the size of the civilian working force than was shown by
the corresponding projection to 1960.

Components of Change Among the Various Occupations

The total working force increases in size via new entries and decreases via
deaths and retirements.   Individual occupations are not only affected by these three

---

3. See annual reports of the National Office of Vital Statistics, Public Health Service,
U. S. Department of Health, Education and Welfare.

components but are also affected by mobility into or out of them.[4] Accordingly the
pattern of change for a major occupation group is much more complex than it is for the
entire working force. During the 1930s and 1940s there was great variation among the
different major occupation groups with respect to the relative importance of these four
components. Accordingly let us examine these changes in some detail in this section.
For our summary purposes it is only necessary to review the experiences of the historical decades of the 1930s and 1940s. It is not necessary to summarize the projected
changes for the 1950s, since we designed our models to reproduce the conditions of these
two past decades; hence the pattern of changes within each major occupation group will
parallel more or less the pattern of changes during the 1930s or 1940s. The one factor
which precludes complete parallelism is that of the changing age distribution; this,
however, seems to have but a slight impact upon the occupational distribution of the
potential manpower supply.

   <u>Accessions to occupations</u>. Accessions are composed: (a) of persons entering
the working force for the first time and obtaining jobs in a given occupation, and (b)
of men already in the working force who move into one occupation from another. The
relative importance of these two elements varies considerably from occupation to occupation.

   In the following occupation groups (Table 6) accessions came almost entirely
from among youths who were first entering the working force; they experienced virtually
no net in-mobility:

   Clerical and kindred workers
   Sales workers
   Operatives and kindred workers
   Farm laborers and foremen
   Laborers, except farm and mine

   Accessions via net in-mobility (rather than new entries into the working
force) were of prime importance for the group of "managers, officials and proprietors,
except farm."

   In the remaining four major occupation groups both elements were important
in contributing to accessions:

   Professional, technical and kindred workers - both of equal importance
   Craftsmen, foremen and kindred workers - (Net in-mobility was somewhat more im-
     portant in periods of prosperity than in depression.)
   Farmers and farm managers, and)
   Service workers   )⁻ (In both these groups net in-mobility was some-
     what less important in periods of prosperity than in depression.)

   In general those major occupation groups in which youths predominate (see
Table 4) are the ones in which the accessions came mainly or exclusively through new
entries into the working force; whatever amount of in-mobility there may have been was
canceled by out-mobility. These occupations tend to be those requiring a minimum amount
of training or skill, thereby making it easier for youths to enter them. Subsequently
as these youths become older and more experienced, they tend to move into the occupations listed above, for which net in-mobility is an important factor in accessions.
These latter occupation groups in general contain the jobs which (as we shall see subsequently) provide higher earnings.

---

4. See also Chapter 7, "Patterns of Working Life."

TABLE 6
COMPONENTS OF CHANGE IN MALE WORKING FORCE
(AGED 4-74 YEARS AS OF BEGINNING OF DECADE)
BY OCCUPATION, 1930-40, 1940-50 AND 1950-60
(Numbers in Thousands)

	1930 to 1940	1940 to 1950	1950 to 1960 A	A'	B	B'
Professional, Technical and Kindred Workers						
Number at beginning of decade	1709.5	2242.8	3080.4	3080.4	3080.4	3080.4
Changes during decade						
New entries	372.6	488.1	386.4	359.9	470.8	433.3
Deaths	260.8	223.7	280.8	280.8	280.8	280.8
Net mobility	+510.3	+684.1	+446.0	+446.0	+584.7	+584.7
Retirements	88.8	110.9	160.9	160.9	141.8	141.8
Additional entries*			142.0	142.0	168.6	168.6
Sum of net changes	+533.3	+837.6	+532.7	+506.2	+801.5	+764.0
Number at end of decade	2242.8	3080.4	3613.1	3586.6	3881.9	3844.4
Clerical and Kindred Workers						
Number at beginning of decade	2092.0	2286.4	2750.7	2750.7	2750.7	2750.7
Changes during decade						
New entries	666.1	819.5	692.1	643.5	860.8	802.3
Deaths	249.0	176.7	231.5	231.5	231.5	231.5
Net mobility	-124.8	- 92.7	-234.4	-234.4	-229.1	-229.1
Retirements	97.9	85.8	198.3	198.3	132.9	132.9
Additional entries*			23.0	23.0	52.8	52.8
Sum of net changes	+194.4	+464.3	+ 50.9	+ 2.3	+320.1	+261.6
Number at end of decade	2268.4	2750.7	2801.6	2753.0	3070.8	3012.3
Operatives and Kindred Workers						
Number at beginning of decade	5802.2	7168.5	8743.6	8743.6	8743.6	8743.6
Changes during decade						
New entries	2085.3	2456.2	2162.1	2006.6	2593.4	2415.1
Deaths	719.6	524.3	648.0	648.0	648.0	648.0
Net mobility	+300.6	-103.0	+ 17.8	+ 17.8	-570.4	-570.4
Retirements	300.0	283.8	607.5	607.5	419.5	419.5
Additional entries*			197.2	197.2	224.0	224.0
Sum of net changes	+1366.3	+1575.1	+1121.6	+966.1	+1179.5	+1001.2
Number at end of decade	7168.5	8743.6	9865.2	9709.7	9923.1	9744.8
Laborers Except Farm and Mine						
Number at beginning of decade	4981.6	4906.3	3690.0	3690.0	3690.0	3690.0
Changes during decade						
New entries	1589.8	1283.7	1655.7	1543.0	1372.1	1290.5
Deaths	709.4	420.7	344.6	344.6	344.6	344.6
Net mobility	-562.7	-1681.7	-519.0	-519.0	-1256.0	-1256.0
Retirements	393.0	397.6	363.5	363.5	341.2	341.2
Additional entries*			55.9	55.9	30.1	30.1
Sum of net changes	- 75.3	-1216.3	+484.5	+371.8	-539.6	-621.2
Number at end of decade	4906.3	3690.0	4174.5	4061.8	3150.4	3068.8

1930 to 1940	1940 to 1950	1950 to 1960			
		A	A'	B	B'

Farmers and Farm Managers

1930 to 1940	1940 to 1950	A	A'	B	B'
627.0	5092.1	4225.5	4225.5	4225.5	4225.5
624.1	509.7	648.2	606.3	505.2	469.6
959.4	820.3	664.7	664.7	664.7	664.7
338.5	+96.0	+336.9	+336.9	+85.7	+85.7
538.1	652.0	404.2	404.2	499.6	499.6
		151.5	151.5	123.8	123.8
534.9	-866.6	+67.7	+25.8	-449.6	-485.2
092.1	4225.5	4293.2	4251.3	3775.9	3740.3

Managers, Officials and Proprietors Except Farm

1930 to 1940	1940 to 1950	A	A'	B	B'
3570.6	3411.1	4374.4	4374.4	4374.4	4374.4
271.5	297.6	280.3	262.2	284.3	261.6
653.6	483.4	571.6	571.6	571.6	571.6
+581.8	+1453.5	+499.6	+499.6	+1324.9	+1324.9
359.2	304.4	512.6	512.6	368.7	368.7
		159.6	159.6	168.6	168.6
-159.5	+963.3	-144.7	-162.8	+837.5	+814.2
3411.1	4374.4	4229.7	4211.6	5211.9	5188.6

Sales Workers

1930 to 1940	1940 to 1950	A	A'	B	B'
138.0	2340.4	2713.0	2713.0	2713.0	2713.0
617.1	705.7	634.9	583.5	742.1	683.6
299.9	212.6	238.8	238.8	238.8	238.8
23.1	-11.8	-55.1	-55.1	-111.8	-111.8
137.9	108.7	208.3	208.3	136.8	136.8
		65.0	65.0	63.0	63.0
202.4	+372.6	+197.7	+146.3	+317.7	+259.2
340.4	2713.0	2910.7	2859.3	3030.7	2972.2

Craftsmen, Foremen and Kindred Workers

1930 to 1940	1940 to 1950	A	A'	B	B'
6128.3	5963.6	8076.2	8076.2	8076.2	8076.2
949.7	1234.1	989.7	927.2	1237.3	1144.2
959.2	697.7	843.5	843.5	843.5	843.5
+315.2	+2010.2	+247.2	+247.2	+1784.5	+1784.5
470.4	434.0	760.5	760.5	566.1	566.1
		231.5	231.5	289.1	289.1
-164.7	+2112.6	-135.6	-198.1	+1901.3	+1808.2
5963.6	8076.2	7940.6	7878.1	9977.5	9884.4

Service Workers

1930 to 1940	1940 to 1950	A	A'	B	B'
794.8	2391.0	2622.5	2622.5	2622.5	2622.5
514.7	503.0	534.0	491.4	559.9	519.1
299.9	279.1	369.2	369.2	369.2	369.2
477.9	+111.3	+493.8	+493.8	+57.2	+57.2
96.5	103.7	197.3	197.3	150.7	150.7
		70.5	70.5	38.5	38.5
96.2	+231.5	+531.8	+489.2	+135.7	+94.9
91.0	2622.5	3154.3	3111.7	2758.2	2717.4

Farm Laborers and Foremen

1930 to 1940	1940 to 1950	A	A'	B	B'
3604.3	3281.7	2120.4	2120.4	2120.4	2120.4
2046.7	1616.7	2085.3	1945.2	1785.1	1692.4
338.7	182.9	140.6	140.6	140.6	140.6
-1859.9	-2465.9	-1232.8	-1232.8	-1669.7	-1669.7
170.7	129.2	122.2	122.2	110.6	110.6
		5.6	5.6	3.6	3.6
-322.6	-1161.3	+595.3	+455.2	-132.2	-224.9
3281.7	2120.4	2715.7	2575.6	1988.2	1895.5

Estimated number of men who were in the armed forces or who were veterans not in the civilian working force in 1950, but who can be expected to have entered the civilian working force by 1960. See Chapter 15 for further information.

Withdrawals from occupations. Net mobility out of an occupation, retirements
from the working force, and deaths all can contribute to men leaving an occupation
(Table 6). These three components were of differing importance among the various occupations. In general we can reason as follows. If an occupation is one from which most
of the men move out as is the case with some occupations, then obviously few men remain
in it long enough to die or retire. On the other hand, if it is not an occupation of
large net out-mobility, then the men leave it via either death or retirement. The relative importance of deaths versus retirements in such cases will be a function of the
retirement rate.[5] As we shall see in Chapter 6, retirement rates vary considerably by
occupation; hence there must be differences among the occupations with respect to the
varying importance of these two components.

An additional consideration bearing on the relationship of deaths to retirements should be kept in mind. As seen previously, there were many more deaths than retirements in the entire working force; in the decade 1940 to 1950 there were about one
and one-half times as many deaths as retirements. Consequently we can expect that in
every occupation deaths ought to be either more numerous, or at least as numerous, as
retirements.

In two major occupation groups, in both the 1930s and 1940s, most of the withdrawals were via net out-mobility; men generally did not remain in them long enough to
reach the retirement age or die. These were:

        Farm laborers and foremen
        Laborers, except farm and mine

Among clerical workers there was some net out-mobility, amounting to about
one fourth of the total number of withdrawals. Of those who did not move out, the great
majority died since the retirement rate for this occupation was relatively low (see also
Table 11).

Among the remaining major occupation groups then, deaths and retirements had
to account for almost all of the withdrawals. In general since there were many more
deaths than retirements in the total working force, we find in each occupation a preponderance of deaths. The ratio of deaths to retirements varies among the occupations
from a little less than 1½-to-one to 2-to-one. This variation in the ratios is a function of the differences in retirement rates. Service workers, who had the lowest retirement rate, had the greatest preponderance of deaths. Farmers and farm managers, on
the other hand, had relatively fewer more deaths than retirements (in the 1940s) because
they had a relatively high retirement rate.[6]

Components of change and occupational growth. How are these diverse components - new entries, net mobility and retirement - related to the rates of growth of
the various occupations? These three components are more or less amenable to change
as circumstances may require. Presumably youths and workers can be directed into one
occupation rather than another, if the needs of society and the labor market should so
demand; the rate of retirement is also amenable to change if such should seem to be
necessary. Deaths, on the other hand, are largely beyond the control of the labor
market. To the extent that the death rate for the entire country has decreased, then

---

5. This results from the fact that identical death rates were used for all occupation
groups during the 1940s. In the 1930s identical rates were used for all nonagricultural
occupations and separate rates for the two agricultural occupations. See Chapter 10.

6. See Chapter 6 and Table 11 for further discussion of farmers and farm managers.

all occupations will benefit; the death rate, however, cannot vary in accordance with any possible labor market requirements. Hence it would seem more relevant to inquire about the historical relationship among the three components over which society can exercise some influence, directly or indirectly, with the rate of growth of the various occupations.

In anticipation of findings to be discussed in subsequent chapters we may note briefly here the following rank order correlations for the decade 1940 to 1950:

a. Between the distribution of new entries by occupation and the percentage change in the size of the occupation   -.29

b. Between net mobility and the percentage change in the size of the occupation   +.62

c. Between the retirement rates and the percentage change in the size of the occupation   -.53

It will be recalled that in the entire working force for this decade there were about 9.9 millions of new entries and 2.6 million retirements. Furthermore according to the way in which we calculated net mobility, there were at least 4.5 million men who moved about among the occupations; this is a very minimum figure, however, since it is the net movement and does not take into account gross movements which canceled each other over the decade (see Chapter 13). In short from the strictly numerical viewpoint new entries and mobility were far more important components than were retirements.

Insofar then as the retirements were of lesser numerical importance in contributing to the change in the size of the working force or of any occupation group, the correlation of -.53 observed between retirements and change in size of occupation is of comparatively little importance. There just were not enough retirements to have any real influence on the changes in the size of the occupations.

The components of new entries and net mobility then were more important in contributing to the changes in size of occupations. Of these two the correlation of net mobility was much greater than that of new entries: +.62 versus -.29. Indeed large numbers of the new entries into the working force entered those very major occupation groups which have been declining in size for a number of decades. We can only conclude then that net mobility was the single most important component in influencing the changes in the size of occupation groups between 1940 and 1950.

Summary. The single most important component in determining the rate of growth of an occupation during any decade is the volume and direction of net mobility. Occupations which grow rapidly are those into which there is considerable net mobility. Large numbers of new entries from among youths who are entering the working force is not enough to insure the growth of an occupation. On the other hand, the occupations which either grow slowly or decrease in size do so because of large-scale net out-mobility rather than because youth do not enter them or because of retirements or deaths.

These conclusions apply equally well to periods of prosperity and depression. During prosperous times, however, there is an increased volume of mobility (see Chapter 5); hence growing occupations increase more rapidly than in depression periods, and declining ones decrease faster then in less prosperous times. In short we may generalize by saying that the numbers of new entries, of deaths and of retirements tend to be similar within each major occupation group during periods of prosperity and depression. In contrast the amount and direction of net mobility varies enormously and is of crucial importance in affecting the rate of growth of an occupation and changes in the rate of growth.

Boys often begin to enter the working force on a part-time basis early in life. Delivering newspapers in the mornings, or delivering groceries on Saturdays, or working during vacations from school is quite common practice. Such work is generally of a kind "suitable for boys" and need bear no relationship to the kind of work which the boy hopes to engage in once he enters the working force on a full-time and permanent basis. Indeed until his late teens or early twenties he may move back and forth between being "officially" in and out of the labor force, as this is determined by the procedures employed by the U. S. Census Bureau.[1] For many, if not most, boys there is no demarkation line clearly separating their pre-working force life from their working life. Instead there is a gradual transition from being permanently out of the working force to being permanently in it. For the most part boys under 14 years or thereabouts are more or less permanently out of the working force. By age 25 or thereabouts most men are permanent members of the civilian working force; most of those who happen to be members of the armed forces at this age will enter the civilian working force upon their discharge from the military.

Rates of New Entries Into the Civilian Working Force

The procedures utilized in this study do not permit ascertaining separately entries, withdrawals and re-entries; they provide the net number of entries into the working force (see Chapter 11). With this qualification in mind let us note the rate at which youths entered the working force as of 1950.

At age 14, the census reported that 12.1 percent of the boys were in the working force in 1950 (Table 7). Since children under this age are not considered as eligible for the working force, this figure can be assumed to be the rate of new entries for this age group. Actually of course some of these boys began working at ages younger than 14, and the figure of 12.1 percent represents the accumulation of new entries over the several preceding ages.

At age 15, some 7.6 percent of the boys who were not in the working force entered. This rate of new entries increased until at age 18 about one in every four boys not in the working force entered it. This increase parallels closely the pattern of boys leaving school. At age 14, some 95 percent of all boys were enrolled in school; by age 18, only about 42 percent were enrolled (as of 1950).[2]

The rates of new entries decreased after age 18 until at age 24 only about 13 percent of those not yet in the civilian working force entered it. By this age - 24 years - most of the young men were in the working force. In 1950, 83.0 percent were in the civilian working force; most of the remaining men were either in school or in the armed forces.

In short as of 1950 about half the boys had entered the civilian working force by age 18, and about three quarters had entered by age 22 (Table 7). There appears to have been a significant increase in the average age of entering the civilian working force between 1930 and 1950. As of 1930 about half of the boys had entered the working

---

1. See 1950 U. S. Census of Population, Bulletin P-C1, pp. xvii ff. See also A. J. Jaffe and Charles Stewart, Manpower Resources and Utilization, Appendix C; Louis J. Ducoff and Margaret Hagood, Social Science Research Council Bulletin 56, "Labor Force Definition and Measurement," New York, 1947.

2. See also A. J. Jaffe and Charles Stewart, Manpower Resources and Utilization, pp. 138-140; 166-168; 355, 356; 375-380; for a fuller discussion of some of the factors and considerations involved in determining the age of entry of boys into the working force.

TABLE 7

RATES OF NEW ENTRIES INTO MALE WORKING FORCE (AGES 14 TO 24), 1950

Age	New entry rate per 100 not in working force[a]	Percent of total population in working force[a]	Percent enrolled in school[b]
14	12.1	12.1	94.7
15	7.6	18.8	91.5
16	11.0	27.7	80.6
17	17.2	40.1	67.9
18	24.0	54.5	42.4
19	18.0	62.7	27.8
20	10.5	66.6	21.2
21	17.4	72.4	19.6
22	16.7	77.0	19.2
23	15.2	80.5	17.6
24	12.8	83.0	15.5

a. Obtained by smoothing the reported numbers in the working force by age and the reported populations.
b. See Chapter 11.
Source: 1950 U. S. Census of Population, P-C 1, Table III.

TABLE 8

PERCENTAGE DISTRIBUTION OF NEW ENTRIES INTO MALE WORKING FORCE
(AGE AS OF BEGINNING OF DECADE) BY AGE AND OCCUPATION, 1930-40 AND 1940-50

	1930 to 1940					1940 to 1950				
	5-9 Years	10-14 Years	15-19 Years	20-24 Years	5-24 Years	5-9 Years	10-14 Years	15-19 Years	20-24 Years	5-24 Years
Professional, technical and kindred workers	0.9	3.2	6.6	11.6	3.9	1.8	4.1	7.1	14.7	4.9
Farmers and farm managers	2.4	5.5	10.5	15.8	6.4	3.0	4.4	7.1	10.4	5.2
Managers, officials and proprietors, except farm	0.5	2.1	5.1	11.4	2.8	0.9	2.4	4.4	10.7	3.0
Clerical and kindred workers	5.9	7.9	6.5	1.2	6.9	7.1	8.6	9.2	5.8	8.3
Sales workers	6.9	6.1	6.2	6.2	6.3	9.6	6.3	5.6	5.4	6.8
Craftsmen, foremen and kindred workers	4.4	8.8	15.4	18.5	9.8	6.1	12.1	16.4	23.4	12.6
Operatives and kindred workers	17.2	22.8	22.9	22.2	21.5	21.0	25.6	27.9	25.1	25.3
Service workers	6.1	5.0	5.0	7.0	5.3	7.9	4.9	3.5	2.1	5.0
Farm laborers and foremen	38.3	21.4	6.5	-	20.7	28.2	18.0	6.3	-	15.9
Laborers except farm and mine	17.3	17.2	15.4	6.1	16.4	14.5	13.6	12.4	2.4	13.0
All occupations	99.9	100.0	100.1	100.0	100.0	100.1	100.0	99.9	100.0	100.0

by age 17, and three quarters had entered by age 19. As of 1940 half of the boys had
entered by about age 18 and three quarters by about age 20½. These figures are summarized as follows:

Census year	Age at which half had entered working force	Age at which three quarters had entered working force
1930	17	19
1940	18	20½
1950	18	22

Whether this trend toward older average age of entry into the working force
will continue into the future cannot be said with certainty. What is certain is that if
most of the youths should serve in the armed forces before entering the civilian working
force, then the average age will continue to rise. If more and more older boys and young
men should continue to go to school, this also may contribute toward an increase in the
age of entering the working force. Since 1950 there has been some increase in school attendance as follows:

Age	Percent enrolled in school[3]		Change
	October 1953	October 1950	
14 and 15 years	96.4	95.2	+1.2
16 and 17 years	76.5	72.8	+3.7
18 and 19 years	37.7	35.2	+2.5
20 to 24 years	18.5	14.2	+4.3

Of course school attendance does not preclude completely participation in the working
force. Nevertheless if the trend toward increased school enrollment should continue,
the average age of entry into the civilian working force will be increased somewhat.

New Entries by Occupation

One factor stands out clearly: the occupations which boys enter are related
to the age of entry into the working force (see Appendix Table 2). We may generalize
by saying that the younger they are the greater is the tendency to enter an occupation
which requires a minimum of education, training or skill. This can be seen by examination of the information about new entries during the decade 1940 to 1950; we may classify
these new entries by age as of 1940 and obtain the following age cohort groups:

Age in 1940	Average age in decade	Age in 1950
5 to 9 years	10 to 14 years	15 to 19 years
10 to 14 years	15 to 19 years	20 to 24 years
15 to 19 years	20 to 24 years	25 to 29 years
20 to 24 years	25 to 29 years	30 to 34 years

We may then note the numbers of each age cohort who entered each of the major occupation
groups during this decade and inquire as to the modal age cohort for each occupation.
For example, consider the group "professional, technical and kindred" occupations; the
numbers of each age cohort who entered during the 1940s were as follows:

---

3. Current Population Reports, U. S. Bureau of the Census, Series P-20, No. 52, January
22, 1954, Table 1. Note that these estimates for October, 1950, are not identical with
the data obtained from the 1950 U. S. Census of Population, P-C1, Table iii, as of April,
1950.

Average age in decade	Number of new entries
10 to 14 years	38,000
15 to 19 years	172,200
20 to 24 years	219,000
25 to 29 years	54,500

It is clear that the single largest group of new entries came from the cohort 20 to 24 years of age. In a similar manner we can analyze the ten major groups with the following results:

Single largest group of new entries from cohort age 20 to 24 years

      Professional, technical and kindred workers
      Farmers and farm managers
      Managers, officials and proprietors, except farm

Single largest group of new entries from cohort age 15 to 19 years

      Clerical and kindred workers
      Sales workers
      Operatives and kindred workers
      Service workers
      Farm laborers and foremen
      Laborers, except farm and mine

New entries into the group "craftsmen, foremen and kindred workers" were equally divided between the groups aged 15 to 19 years and 20 to 24 years.

The diverse patterns of new entries by age and occupation are seen clearly in Table 8 showing the percentage distribution of new entries. For the decade 1940 to 1950 the youngest age group, those 5 to 9 years in 1940, entered the groups "farm laborers and foremen," "operatives and kindred workers," and "laborers, except farm and mine"; these three categories accounted for two thirds of all the new entries.

In the next older age group, those 10 to 14 years in 1940, the leading occupational group was "operatives and kindred workers"; about one quarter of all the boys entered this occupation. "Farm laborers and foremen" was the second largest group. The two groups, "laborers, except farm and mine" and "craftsmen, foremen and kindred workers" had almost equal numbers of new entries from this age group. These four groups accounted for about two thirds of all the new entries.

In the next older age group, 15 to 19 years in 1940, the leading occupational category was "operatives and kindred workers" followed by "craftsmen, foremen and kindred workers" and "laborers, except farm and mine." Very few boys were entering "farm laborers and foremen"; indeed more entered the category "professional, technical and kindred workers" than became farm laborers.

Finally in the oldest age group about one quarter of the new entries went into "operatives and kindred workers" and one quarter into "craftsmen, foremen and kindred workers." Another third of the young men entered white collar occupations. None became "farm laborers and foremen."

These patterns can be summarized as follows:

Percent of new entries into	Age in 1940				
	5 to 9 years	10 to 14 years	15 to 19 years	20 to 24 years	5 to 24 years
White collar occupations	19.4	21.4	26.3	36.6	23.0
Craftsmen, foremen and kindred	6.1	12.1	16.4	23.4	12.6
Other manual, except farm	43.4	44.1	43.8	29.6	43.3
Agriculture	31.2	22.4	13.4	10.4	21.1

-Considering together the four age groups, we note that in the 1940s about 25 percent of the new entries went into "operatives and kindred workers," about 16 percent into "farm laborers and foremen," and 13 percent each into "craftsmen, foremen and kindred workers" and "laborers, except farm and mine." About 15 percent became clerical and sales workers, 5 percent "professional, technical and kindred workers," and only 3 percent "managers, officials and proprietors, except farm." Clearly this distribution of new entries (Table 8) did not correspond to the occupational distribution of all civilian male workers (Table 1). As we shall see, as these men become older, they will experience considerable occupational mobility, and they will rearrange themselves into a different occupational distribution (Chapter 5).

Occupational Distribution of New Entries in the 1930s as Compared With the 1940s

The patterns of new entries by occupation and age as described previously for the 1940s also prevailed during the 1930s. In general also the distribution of all new entries in both decades tended to be substantially similar. In both decades, for example, the occupation group which received the largest number of new entries was that of "operatives and kindred workers"; that occupation which received the smallest number of new entries was that of "managers, officials and proprietors, except farm."

There were a number of differences between the two decades, however, which seem attributable in part to the differences in economic conditions and in part to the continuation of the long-time trends in occupational shifts in the United States. The decrease in the proportion of all new entries who went into agriculture between these two decades, for example, is in part a continuation of the long-time trends away from agriculture. In part also it is a reflection of the fact that during the 1930s many boys were unable to obtain nonagricultural employment and had to remain as farm laborers, very often on their relatives' farms.

The increase in the proportion who went into the white collar occupations also reflects the dual impacts of long-time trends in occupational shifts toward more white collar workers, together with the fact that such jobs were more plentiful during the 1940s than they had been during the preceding decade.

On the other hand, the increase in the proportion of new entries into the category "craftsmen, foremen and kindred workers" clearly reflects the impact of the prosperity of the 1940s and the greatly increased demand for such workers then. Similarly the increase in the proportion who went into "operatives and kindred workers" reflected the demand situation of the 1940s for such workers.

The difference between these two decades can be summarized as follows:

Percent of new entries into	1930 to 1940	1940 to 1950	Change
White collar occupations	19.9	23.0	+3.1
Craftsmen, foremen and kindred workers	9.8	12.6	+2.8
Other manual, except farm	43.2	43.3	+0.1
Agriculture	27.1	21.1	-6.0

The groups of occupations in the heading "other manual, except farm" seem to have remained unchanged during these two decades. Actually there was a substantial increase in the group "operatives and kindred workers" accompanied by decreases in the proportions who entered the service category and "laborers except farm and mine." These diverse changes just canceled each other between the periods 1930 to 1940 and 1940 to 1950.

Factors Associated With the Distribution of New Entries

The question may be raised regarding the reasons why boys enter these occupations in accordance with the patterns described above. We could assume the hypothesis of a flexible labor supply which adapts itself to the demands of the labor market and to changes in such demand patterns. If this assumption is made, then we should say that new entries would go into the growing occupations; that the number of men in an occupation is increasing over the years can be taken as an indication that the demand for such workers is increasing.

However, it would seem that the expanding or increasing occupations tend to be those which require more education, training or other skills; there is some evidence that this has been the case historically in the United States.[4] Furthermore these jobs which require more training or skills - whether the skills be that of a machinist or certified public accountant or business or professional man - are also the jobs which tend to provide larger earnings.

Youths entering the working force for the first time are for the most part ill equipped to fill the demand for such better jobs.[5] Some of them will have acquired the necessary training in schools, but much of the skills needed for these better jobs can be acquired only via on-the-job training of some sort. A certified public accountant, for example, often will have received some of his training from a college and some by working as a bookkeeper. Accordingly many, if not most, youths are unable to enter these better jobs, which also tend to be the growing occupations. They are forced, one might almost say, to enter those jobs which require but a minimum of experience and are therefore easy to enter. These occupations tend to be those which are slower growing or even declining in numbers.

Some confirmation for this can be seen by examining the occupational distribution of the new entries during the decade 1940 to 1950. This was a period of full employment, and presumably the youths could have entered any occupations which they were capable of filling. We noted previously the occupations which they did enter. What do we know about these occupations? We know several attributes of these occupational groups as follows: the percent change in number of workers between 1940 and 1950, the median number of years schooling which the men in these occupations had (as of 1950), and the median income earned in 1949. The first attribute can be taken as a measure of the variable demand for workers in the several occupations. The two other attributes can be combined into a measure of the quality of the job denoting the relative amount of training and education required.

These two measures of the occupation can then be correlated (by means of rank correlations) with the occupational distribution of new entries during the 1940s.

---

4. See, for example, Jaffe and Stewart, Manpower, "Changes in Skill Levels," pp. 193 ff.

5. See also Gladys Palmer, Labor Mobility in Six Cities, Chapter 5, "Relative Ease of Entry to Occupations and Industries," p. 91.

The correlation between occupational distribution and percent change in size of occupation between 1940 and 1950 was -.29. This correlation is small and not of much significance, but it does suggest that the new entries did not flow automatically into the expanding occupations.

The correlation between occupational distribution of new entries and the quality of the job was -.47. This correlation, although small, suggests a tendency to enter those occupations which require lesser experience and training.

The correlation between percentage change in size of occupation between 1940 and 1950 and the quality of the job (as measured by education and income) was +.86. It seems fairly clear that in this decade at least the expanding occupations were the better ones, i.e., those requiring more skills and offering higher earnings.[6]

We can now calculate the correlation between the occupational distribution of the new entries and the percent change in size of occupation while removing (or partialing out) the influence of the quality of the occupation. When this is done, the correlation becomes +.27. This suggests some tendency for the new entries to go into the expanding occupations, at least to the extent to which they are qualified to do so.

In summary boys tend to enter those occupations which are easiest to enter because they require comparatively less schooling or other training and skills, and little if any capital investment. Subsequently as they become older, many of them acquire the necessary skills and training, or the necessary capital if they intend to open a business or operate a farm, and leave their earlier jobs for these better jobs. Occupational mobility moves these men up, and sometimes down, the occupational ladder.

---

6. Note that a job actually may not require as much skill or training as an employer thinks it does. For some particular job a high school graduate, for example, may be just as competent as a college graduate. If the employer thinks that he must have a college graduate, however, then the actual skill level for that job, insofar as the employer and job applicant are concerned, is that of a college graduate.

CHAPTER 5
NET MOBILITY

Having reviewed the information on the occupations which young men enter when they first become members of the working force, let us now follow them through their subsequent occupational histories. The one point that is clear is that the initial job is not necessarily the individual's lifetime job; rather he moves about from occupation to occupation as he is able and circumstances permit. As a result of such mobility the occupational distribution of men in the older ages bears but a minor resemblance to the occupational distribution with which these men began their working careers. Such gross changes can be observed readily enough by noting the occupational distribution of a specific age cohort even over a space of time as short as 20 years. Thus we might compare the occupational distribution of men aged 15 to 24 years in 1930 with the occupational pattern of the same men in 1950 when the survivors were 35 to 44 years of age.

| | Percentage distribution | |
	1930	1950
Professional, technical and kindred workers	2.9	6.8
Farmers and farm managers	5.2	12.6
Managers, officials and proprietors, except farm	2.5	11.0
Clerical and kindred workers	8.9	5.5
Sales workers	5.8	6.1
Craftsmen, foremen and kindred workers	10.4	18.4
Operatives and kindred workers	19.6	18.2
Service workers	3.8	6.2
Farm laborers and foremen	24.7	4.3
Laborers except farm and mine	16.2	10.9
Total	100.0	100.0

Inspection of these pictures of the occupational distribution of the same men taken twenty years apart clearly indicate that substantial mobility has occurred. Obviously there was considerable net mobility into the groups:

Professional, technical and kindred workers
Farmers and farm managers
Managers, officials and proprietors, except farm
Craftsmen, foremen and kindred workers
Service workers

There was also considerable net mobility out of:

Clerical and kindred workers
Farm laborers and foremen
Laborers except farm and mine

With respect to the two remaining groups, sales workers and operatives, perhaps in- and out-mobility almost balanced each other.

Definition of Mobility Rates

The detailed explanation of occupational mobility rates is given in Chapter 13. In the present chapter we want to remind the reader that we are trying to measure only relative levels of mobility both as among the occupations and age groups, and over time. Our procedures did not permit ascertaining any absolute levels of mobility. Indeed there is considerable question whether there are any absolute levels of occupational mobility. It can be argued that such absolute levels could exist to be measured only if there were a fixed and finite number of mutually exclusive occupations. Actually there are, or can be, almost an infinite number of different occupations. How many there may be in any particular classification scheme depends upon how one desires to arrange the infinite variety of ways in which people earn their livings.[1]

Occupational mobility can occur only when someone changes his occupation or the way in which he earns his living. Hence the number of different occupations established and the definition of each, and consequently the definition of what constitutes a change in occupation, contribute toward determining the amount of mobility which can occur. It follows then that, since there is no uniquely correct number or classification of occupations, there can be no uniquely correct levels of occupational mobility. In short only relative levels of mobility can be measured. If the same measuring procedures are used for several time periods or several populations, then we compare the relative amounts of mobility among them.

We also wish to remind our readers that, unless otherwise specified, we are measuring net mobility, i.e., the difference between the number of in movements and out movements. Our models and the data available did not permit separate measurement of the amounts of in and out movements. Furthermore we can measure net movements only into or out of an occupation; we were unable to measure the relative exchange between any two given occupation groups.[2]

Total Mobility Rates

By definition the total amount of mobility as among the various occupations must be zero; this is to say that the amount of in-mobility must equal and cancel the amount of out-mobility.[3] If we take then the total amount of in-mobility during a decade and divide it by the number of men in the working force at the end of the decade, we have a measure of the relative levels of occupational mobility for all occupations combined. If this is done by five-year age groups, we have measures of the relative amounts of occupational mobility by age.

Examination of such rates by age reveals a general pattern as follows. In the very youngest age cohort (age 5 to 9 years at the beginning of the decade and 15 to 19 years at the end of the decade) the level of mobility is quite low. With increasing age men become much more occupationally mobile; the peak is reached at the age level of 15 to 24 years (at the beginning of the decade and 25 to 34 years at the end of the decade). After this the rates decrease fairly consistently and become negligible at the older ages (Table 9). Indeed beyond about the age of 50 years (as of the beginning of the decade) the amount of mobility is so small in comparison with the numbers of retirements and deaths that net mobility can be discounted as an important factor in making projections for individual occupations.

---

1. Herbert S. Parnes, Social Science Research Council Bulletin 65, see especially Chapter 2, "The Problem of Classifying Labor Mobility."

2. It should be borne in mind that for the purposes of making the projections to 1960, which was the main goal of this study, it was not necessary to specify either the amount of gross mobility nor the interchange as between any two occupations. The essential figure which had to be determined was about how much an occupation might grow or decline in the decade due to net in- or out-mobility. If it had been easy to devise models and obtain data which would have provided gross mobility and the amount of movement between any two occupations, such would have been done; this, however, turned out to be impossible to do.

3. We are assuming a closed universe with no foreign migration. This was virtually the case in the United States in the period 1930 to 1950.

TABLE 9

TOTAL MOBILITY RATES FOR ALL OCCUPATION GROUPS COMBINED
(AGE AS OF BEGINNING OF DECADE)
1930-40 AND 1940-50

| Age | Male Working Force[a] | | Six City Study[b] |
	1930 to 1940	1940 to 1950	1940 to 1950
5 to 9 years	.010	.011	-
10 to 14 years	.067	.113	-
15 to 19 years	.160	.212	.247
20 to 24 years	.157	.211	.215
25 to 29 years	.084	.162	.133
30 to 34 years	.051	.113	.079
35 to 39 years	.031	.079	.063
40 to 44 years	.028	.059	.056
45 to 49 years	.021	.050	.092
50 to 54 years	.021	.029	.049
55 to 59 years	.027	.025	.065
60 to 64 years	.048	.010	.096

a. Total in-mobility in all occupations combined, divided by total number
expected in the working force at the end of the decade.

b. Source: Special Tabulation of Six City Study.
    Rate calculated by dividing the total in-mobility for all occupations
combined by the total number in the working force at the end of the decade.

Comparison of the patterns of mobility rates for the 1930s and 1940s reveals them to be virtually identical in almost all respects (Chart 1). The apparent irregularities observed among the older age groups in the 1930s may have resulted as much from irregularities in the basic data as from any actual variations in the mobility rates (see Chapter 9).

The only real difference between the rates for the 1930s and those for the 1940s is the level. At all ages (except the very youngest and the two oldest cohorts) the rates during the later decade are significantly above those of the earlier decade. This difference corresponds to the differences in the economic conditions of the two decades. The prosperity of the 1940s together with the attendant labor shortages led to considerable movement of workers as among the various occupations. By contrast the "over sufficiency" of labor supply during the 1930s, in comparison with the demand pattern, was not conducive to job changing.[4]

For comparative purposes we have included in Table 9 the mobility rates by age as calculated from the data of the Six City Study. Because of the totally different way in which this Six City Study was conducted, the levels of these rates are not comparable with those which we calculated. Only the patterns of rates by age in the two studies might be compared. In general the two studies show rather similar patterns of occupational mobility by age. The largest difference is among the older age groups, where the rates from the Six City Study appear to fluctuate somewhat more than ours do.[5]

Mobility Rates by Occupation

From our previous discussion of this topic it is clear that the differences in net mobility as among the various major occupation groups are large and of considerable importance in affecting the differential rates of growth of the occupations. This conclusion is graphically portrayed in Chart 2.

The ten major occupation groups can be subdivided into several patterns of occupational mobility by age. In three occupations there was net in-mobility at almost all ages and in both the 1930s and 1940s. These groups are:

Professional, technical and kindred workers
Managers, officials and proprietors, except farm
Craftsmen, foremen and kindred workers

Two groups were diametrically opposite in that they experienced net out-mobility at almost all ages:

Farm laborers and foremen
Laborers except farm and mine

Considerable net in-mobility in the younger ages accompanied by considerable net out-mobility in the older ages in both decades was characteristic of two groups:

---

4. Herbert S. Parnes, Social Science Research Council Bulletin 65, Chapter 4, "Factors Affecting Labor Mobility," see section "The Level of Business Activity."

5. See Chapter 16 for a comparison of the Six City Study with our study.

Farmers and farm managers
Operatives and kindred workers

Relatively little net in-mobility at the youngest ages, followed by large-scale net out-mobility in the middle ages, with little mobility at the oldest ages, was characteristic of the groups:

Clerical and kindred workers
Sales workers

Mobility in the group of service workers is perhaps most influenced by economic conditions. During depression periods this occupation experienced net in-mobility at all ages. During the prosperous 1940s, however, there was considerable net out-mobility in the younger ages, followed by net in-mobility in the older ages.

These patterns can be generalized somewhat as follows. The maximum mobility, whether in or out, tended to occur at the younger ages. Although there were differences as among the various occupation groups, we might say that by age 40 or thereabouts the volume of net mobility had diminished considerably.

Comparison of the Two Decades

Comparison of the two decades reveals a tendency toward larger net mobility rates (whether in or out) at most ages for all occupation groups during the 1940s. In short the increased prosperity and labor demand conditions of this decade which led to increased occupational mobility as previously noted (see Chart 1) affected all segments of the working force and was not limited entirely to certain occupations or age groups. It is true that certain age groups and occupations were perhaps more affected by economic conditions than were others, but all groups were affected to some extent.

The over-all effect of the differences in mobility patterns between these two decades was to increase the numbers of the better paying jobs much more than the poorer paying ones. The five occupations with lowest median income (in 1949) all either lost more workers through out-mobility in the 1940s as compared with the 1930s, or gained far fewer workers via in-mobility. On the other hand, the largest increases in the volume of in-mobility occurred among the better paying jobs.

Factors Associated With Mobility Levels

The volume and direction of net mobility during the 1940s was associated clearly with the expanding occupations, and the better ones. As a measure of the importance of net mobility in each occupation we can divide the volume of net mobility by the number of men in the occupation in 1940 (using the data shown in Table 6). We can note also the direction of the net movement and rank the occupations beginning with that which had the largest percentage of net in-mobility and ending with that which had the largest percentage of net out-mobility. These two extreme occupations were "managers, officials and proprietors, except farm" and "farm laborers and foremen."

We can then correlate these ranks with the rank order of percentage change in occupation size between 1940 and 1950. When this is done, we obtain a correlation of +.62. Obviously there was a tendency for mobility into the faster expanding occupations and out of the more slowly expanding or declining occupations. Perhaps the main reason why the correlation was not higher was because of the tendency of new entries to go into many of the occupations which did not grow during the decade. As we noted previously, new entries tended to go into those occupations which required less skill and training and therefore were easiest of access. Subsequently very many of them moved out of these occupations and into better jobs. The figures on percentage change in occupation size, however, include the new entries and therefore reduce the relationship between net mobility and total occupation growth.

We can also correlate the rank order of volume of mobility with the quality of the occupation as previously described.[6] This index combines the educational level of the men in the occupation with the median total income in 1949. This correlation was +.73. Clearly the mobility was toward the better jobs.

Furthermore as we noted previously, there was a high correlation, +.86, between quality and rate of growth of the occupation. In short it is quite evident that occupational mobility was of crucial importance in matching labor supply and demand and in moving men into better jobs, i.e., contributing to vertical mobility.

CHART 1. OCCUPATIONAL MOBILITY RATES
(ALL OCCUPATIONS COMBINED)
BY AGE, 1930-40 AND 1940-50

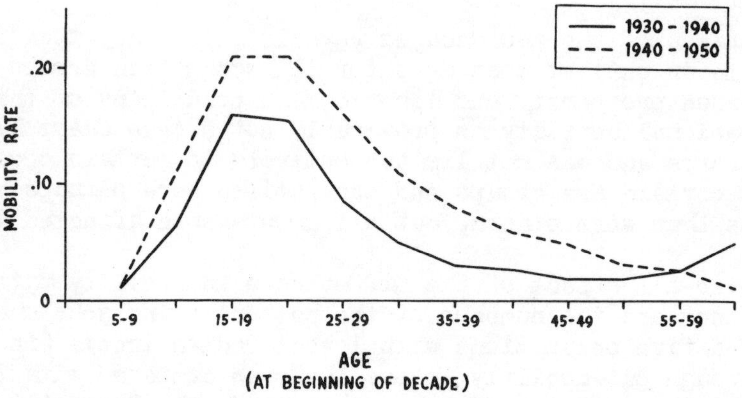

6.   Chapter 4, section on "Factors Associated With the Distribution of New Entries."

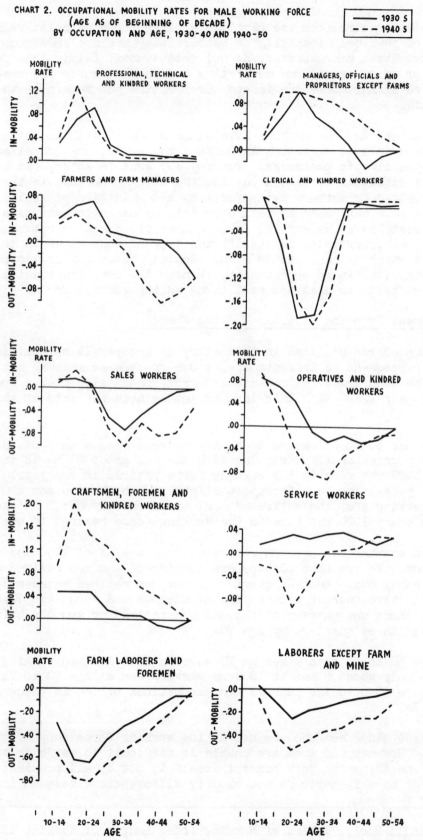

CHART 2. OCCUPATIONAL MOBILITY RATES FOR MALE WORKING FORCE
(AGE AS OF BEGINNING OF DECADE)
BY OCCUPATION AND AGE, 1930-40 AND 1940-50

A few men retire from the civilian working force at relatively young ages, either because of physical disability or because they are not under economic pressure to earn a living. Most men, however, do not retire until fairly late in life, perhaps above 60 years or so of age. Some men retire and then re-enter the working force after which they retire again. Some men indeed never retire but remain in the working force until their death.

Retirements and new entries have at least one factor in common. Boys in our society, as indeed in most societies throughout the world, are compelled to enter the working force by society's pressures. The boy may want to enter, but even if he does not, he finds it difficult to remain outside the working force. At the other end of life men are expelled from the working force by a combination of social and physiological pressures. Whether a man wants to retire or not, he can often exercise but little choice and eventually must leave the working force either via death or retirement. Society provides him with some opportunity to specify the type of work he wants to do and the circumstances under which he cares to do such. Society gives him less opportunity, and disability and death give him no opportunity, to make the more fundamental decision regarding whether he wants to or does not want to be in the working force.

Rates of Retirement From the Civilian Working Force[1]

The procedures utilized in this study do not permit determining retirements, re-entries and subsequent retirements again; our procedures measure net retirements - the difference between gross retirements and gross re-entries over a specified period of time (see Chapter 12). With this in mind let us note the rate at which men retired as of 1950.

Below age 50 there seemed to be so few retirements that no rates were calculated for these younger ages. Beginning with the age group 50 to 54 then, we note that about 7 men in 1000 who were in the working force retired in one year. In the next age group, 55 to 59 years, the rate increased slightly when about 8 per 1000 retired (Table 10). With increasing age, the retirement rate rose sharply until at age 70 to 74 years some 100 men in every 1000 who were in the working force retired in one year.

We can examine the data on retirements by age as of 1950 and note the average age of retirement. We see that perhaps one quarter of the men retired some time between age 50 and the early 60s. Another quarter of the men retired between the early and middle 60s and a third quarter between the middle 60s and about age 70. More precisely we can say that about one quarter of the men had retired by age 62; half had retired by about age 64; and three quarters by age 70.

At age 50 to 54 some 9 men in 10 were in the civilian working force in 1950. At age 60 to 64 only about 8 men in 10 were workers and at age 70 to 74 fewer than 4 men in 10. Beyond age 75 both the numbers and proportions of men in the working force became almost negligible.

Of these older men who are not in the working force many of them are physically unable to work. How many of them are unable is difficult to say with any degree of preciseness. For one thing the very concept itself is not at all precise; for another the census statistics on this topic do not clearly differentiate between inability to work

1. See also Harold Wool, "Tables of Working Life, Length of Working Life of Men," Bureau of Labor Statistics, Bulletin 1001, U. S. Department of Labor, July, 1950.

TABLE 10
RETIREMENT RATES FROM MALE WORKING FORCE BY AGE, 1930, 1940 AND 1950
(Per 1000 Men)*

Age	1930	1940	1950
50 to 54 years	3.8	4.8	7.2
55 to 59 years	8.0	10.5	8.1
60 to 64 years	17.7	31.0	31.7
65 to 69 years	35.2	68.9	67.9
70 to 74 years	66.6	100.9	100.7

* Number estimated to have retired in one year divided by the number in the occupation at the census date plus the number who retired.

TABLE 11
STANDARDIZED RETIREMENT RATES OF MALE WORKING FORCE BY OCCUPATION
1930-40 AND 1940-50
(Per 1000 Men)*

	1930-40	1940-50	Percent of Change
Professional, technical and kindred workers	165	150	-9.1
Farmers and farm managers	160	206	+28.7
Managers, officials and proprietors, except farm	243	180	-26.0
Clerical and kindred workers	232	160	-31.1
Sales workers	240	159	-33.8
Craftsmen, foremen and kindred workers	245	187	-23.7
Operatives and kindred workers	257	187	-27.3
Service workers	132	98	-25.8
Farm laborers and foremen	234	212	-9.5
Laborers except farm and mine	282	267	-5.4
All occupations	222	188	-15.4

* Computed by standardizing the age specific rates shown in Appendix Table 3, on the age distribution of the total male working force in 1940, as estimated to have survived to 1950.

and retirement from the working force while still able to work.[2] At age 70 to 74 years
in 1950, for example, the census reported that:

    37 percent of the men were in the working force
    30 percent were "unable to work"
    3 percent were inmates of institutions
    30 percent were "other," presumably "retired" for the most part

        This pattern of retirement by age as estimated for 1950 was rather similar to
the patterns in 1940 and 1930. In 1930 all of the age specific rates were estimated to
be well below the levels of 1940 and 1950, with the possible exception of the age group
55 to 59 years. The retirement rates for 1940 and 1950, however, were estimated to be
of almost the same level, age for age (Table 10).

        What will happen in the future is difficult to say. It would seem unlikely
that retirement rates will be reduced substantially, since by age 65 or 70 very many men
are physically incapable of doing much work. Of course if part-time work for older men
should become widespread, fewer of them would have to retire "permanently and full time";
we could have widespread "part-time" retirement. Also if medical science should find
cures for many of the diseases of older people and increase the life span substantially,
more older men would probably remain in the working force. Whether such medical dis-
coveries will be made in the very near future, however, is problematical.

        Retirement rates could rise in the future, particularly if the various retire-
ment plans including Old Age and Survivors Insurance should be altered drastically. For
example, if age 55 should become the accepted retirement age, instead of about age 65 as
at present, the retirement rates would increase. Also depression and unemployment would
lead to involuntary retirement and a rise in the over-all retirement rate.

Retirement Rates by Occupation

        During the 1940s about 188 men of every 1000 who had been in the working force
in 1940 retired.[3] The lowest retirement rate was observed among service workers among
whom only some 98 in 1000 retired (Table 11). The highest rate was estimated for the
group "laborers, except farm and mine."

        In addition to the service workers the retirement rates for all the white col-
lar groups were below the rate for the entire working force.

        The two groups:

    Craftsmen, foremen and kindred workers
    Operatives and kindred workers

had retirement rates virtually identical with that of the total working force.

2. See also Jaffe and Stewart, Manpower, pp. 214, 215.

3. This rate was obtained by dividing the total number of retirements estimated to have
occurred between 1940 and 1950 (see Chapter 12) by the number of men in the working
force in 1940 who were estimated to have survived to 1950. For the separate occupations
shown in Table 11 standardized retirement rates were computed by applying the age specific rates shown in Appendix Table 3 to the age distribution of the total male working
force in 1940 as estimated to have survived to 1950.

The two agricultural occupations in addition to the group "laborers, except farm and mine" had retirement rates significantly above that of the total working force.

During the 1930s the retirement rates for all occupation groups with the exception of "farmers and farm managers" were significantly higher than in the 1940s. For six of the occupations the retirement rates decreased from between one quarter and one third over the two decades (Table 11). In three of the occupations the reduction was under 10 percent; these were:

Professional, technical and kindred workers
Farm laborers and foremen
Laborers except farm and mine

Among "farmers and farm managers" the retirement rate, in contrast, increased by about one quarter.

The same general pattern of occupational differences in retirement rates prevailed during the 1930s. Those which had the lowest retirement rates in the 1930s generally continued to have the lowest rates in the later decade; those occupations with the highest rates in the 1930s also had the highest rates in the 1940s. The major exception to this pattern was the group of "farmers and farm managers"; this occupation had the second lowest retirement rate in the earlier decade and the third from the highest in the 1940s.

Examination of the retirement rates by five-year age groups and occupation (Appendix Table 3) reveals the same general pattern of greatly increasing rates with increasing age. The rate for each occupation at the oldest age group (age 60 to 64 years at the beginning of the decade) was many times greater than that for the youngest age group (age 40 to 44 at the beginning of the decade). This pattern is very similar to that previously noted for all occupations combined (see Table 10).

Comparison of the separate age and occupation groups for the two decades reveals declines in the 1940s in almost all rates, with the exception of the "farmers and farm managers." For this group the retirement rate at each age was higher during the 1940s than in the 1930s.

In short it is clear that retirement was more prevalent in the 1930s than in the 1940s with the exception of this one group of farmers. Presumably the lack of employment opportunities in the 1930s contributed to more voluntary and involuntary retirement.

The Retirement of Farmers

Since the farmers experienced such totally different changes in retirement rates during these two decades and since this group had such a relatively high rate during the 1940s (in comparison with the other occupations), let us examine this occupation in rather more detail.

The numbers of men 50 years of age and over, returned by the census as "farmers and farm managers," were as follows:

1930	2,143,000
1940	2,080,000
1950	1,681,000

Between 1930 and 1940 there was a decrease of about 63,000 farmers and between 1940 and 1950 about 399,000. Apparently there was a larger exodus during the 1940s than during the 1930s.

These men could have moved into some other occupation or they could have retired from the working force. Our procedures showed them to have retired rather than to have moved to some other occupation. How likely is it that they experienced net out-mobility rather than retirement? We can reason as follows.

Under ordinary circumstances these older farmers might have become farm laborers. The age specific participation rates for farm laborers as shown by the censuses decreased also over these years, however; therefore it does not seem likely that any large numbers of farmers became farm laborers. Ordinarily also it is unlikely that these older farmers would have entered nonagriculture in great numbers. The early 1940s, however, were unusual times in that there was a very great shortage of labor. Many older men even with a minimum of experience in nonagriculture were able to and did obtain such jobs. Hence perhaps many farmers moved out of agriculture during the years of the Second World War. That this seems to have been the case is suggested by the census information which shows the following numbers of "farmers and farm managers":

1940	5,164,000
1945	4,400,000
1950	4,341,000

Without detailed examination of these numbers by age, we cannot estimate how much of the decline between 1940 and 1945 was occasioned by out-mobility and how much by failure of young men to become farmers. Inspection of the figures, however, do suggest that there must have been out-mobility in this period. Between 1945 and 1950, however, there was almost no change in the numbers of farmers; this suggests that there was no large volume of out-mobility in this later period.

If now many of the older farmers who shifted to nonagriculture in the early 1940s retired from the working force between 1945 and 1950, our procedures would have credited them to the group of "farmers and farm managers" rather than to whatever occupation they had last worked at. In short our procedures relate retirement to the occupation in which the man was at the beginning of the decade. For the purposes of making projections, it was not necessary to determine any mobility which may have occurred in an intercensal period, between the beginning of the decade (i.e., the census date) and the time the man finally retired from the working force.

Factors Associated With Occupational Differences in Retirement Rates

Why are there these differences in retirement rates by occupation? To some extent retirements may be involuntary; the man is forced out of his job and cannot obtain another one. After fruitlessly seeking for work for some time he becomes discouraged and "retires" from the working force. If he is self-employed, simply because there is no employer to order him out of a job, he may continue at his trade for some time, even if he is not earning a living from it. These factors seem to have been operating during the 1930s, and occupational differences in retirement seem to have been accounted for in substantial measure by the depressed conditions of the labor market.[4]

During the 1940s, however, under the conditions of full employment there was probably much less involuntary retirement. Many men were able to obtain employment at pay levels significantly above what their retirement pensions would have been, and as a result they remained in the working force. Accordingly we may ask what the factors are under conditions of full employment that are associated with men retiring from, or remaining in the working force. To answer this question in part, we can correlate the

---

4. Jaffe and Stewart, Manpower, pp. 229 ff.

retirement rates by occupation (as shown in Table 11) with the index of the quality of
the occupation.[5] This correlation is -.67. The retirement rates were lower in those
occupations having the better jobs. This relationship is, in part, a reflection of the
fact that the less desirable jobs are also the ones tending to involve physical work
rather than mental work. Hence older men, being less able physically, have to leave
these occupations. To the extent that physical capabilities are relevant in determining
levels of retirement, then, such men might be considered as involuntarily retired. Perhaps they did not care to retire but could no longer continue to perform the work required by the job. This type of involuntary retirement, to the extent that it may exist,
is quite different from the retirement enforced by large-scale unemployment and the un-
availability of jobs, such as was experienced during the 1930s.

We can also correlate retirement rates with the percentage change in the numbers of men in the occupation between 1940 and 1950. This correlation is -.53. The retirement rates were higher in those occupations which were growing least rapidly, or
perhaps even declining in numbers. To some extent of course the very fact of higher
retirement rates will contribute toward a slower rate of growth of the occupation. On
the other hand, the very fact that an occupation is not growing rapidly indicates that
job opportunities in that occupation are not expanding as rapidly as elsewhere; consequently there may be some pressure on the individual to retire, i.e., involuntary retirement.

We should remember also that the most rapidly expanding occupations were those
having the better jobs. Accordingly there is some reason to believe that the differential retirement rates by occupation, even under conditions of full employment, reflect in
part differential employment opportunities. Those men who are in occupations in relatively declining sectors of the economy tend to be forced out; since they do not have the
training to obtain the better jobs in the expanding sectors of the labor market, they are
simply forced to retire.

The analysis of course tells us nothing about the nature of the desires of the
men with reference to retirement. We only know with some degree of certainty that many
men cannot afford to retire. The Federal Old Age and Survivors Insurance program and
other retirement plans generally pay so much less than the man earns that he takes a
large cut in money income upon retirement; furthermore a number of men are not covered
by retirement plans. Consequently it is not surprising that so many men continue to work
after they become eligible to retire. The crucial question to which we have no answer is
whether they would prefer to retire or prefer to continue working if economic considerations were not so important a factor.

---

5. Chapter 4, section on "Factors Associated With the Distribution of New Entries."

CHAPTER 7
PATTERNS OF WORKING LIFE

Introduction

Up to this point we have been studying the components of occupational change mainly from the point of view of their immediate application for making projections of the occupational distribution. Such was the main aim of this study. In reviewing these components, however, and in noticing their influences upon occupational composition, it became quite clear that we were studying lifetime patterns. We observed, so to speak, the working life of the average man from the time he entered the working force and from occupation to occupation until the time he retired.

Unfortunately we had the opportunity to study such changes only over a twenty-year period since historical data were available only for the period 1930 to 1950. Most men, however, spend 40 to 50 years in the working force, if they live that long; hence our observations actually covered less than half of the working life span of any man or cohort of men. In order to obtain a picture of the complete working life, then, we must combine the experiences of various age groups into a reasonable facsimile of the totality. Some day, perhaps in 1970 or 1980, some future student may review the entire working life of those men who entered the working force in 1930 and trace them through decade by decade until they will have left the working force. He will then produce a correct historical picture of what actually occurred during the entire working life. Until that day comes, synthetic or composite analyses, such as ours, will have to suffice.

In reviewing such working life patterns as we were able to construct, not surprisingly there turned out to be no average man and no single typical working life pattern. Rather there are a number of different types of men who undergo different patterns of working life experiences. The time of entering the working force, the occupational shifts, and the time of retirement all together form discernible patterns and, in so doing, reveal the process of social stratification. It is true of course that social stratification consists of more than occupational distribution and occupational change, but it is contended that working life experiences in our society at least constitute the single most important element in social stratification. Hence by observing the ordered patterns of working life we observe a motion picture of social mobility and the process of social stratification.

Change of occupation or job is characteristic of the American man. Sometimes such change is voluntary and sometimes it is involuntary; sometimes also pure chance seems to play an important role.[1] Nevertheless there appear to be fairly regular patterns which describe the working histories of men. Gladys Palmer refers to this pattern as the "career framework" of an individual. In the case of most men their job changes fall into patterns, and accidental factors seem to play but a minor role. The work histories of the men studied by Dr. Palmer exhibited a rationale whereby what is referred to as "career framework" considerations seem to explain a good many of their job changes.[2] Hence when making projections we need not worry that occupational changes will upset all our estimates. As long as such changes follow regular patterns through life and change with the age of the man, we can project these patterns with reasonable assurance by taking into account the change in the age of the individual.

This last statement should not be interpreted as implying that whatever pattern we may uncover as of the 1940s or 1950s are necessarily "permanent." On the contrary it

---

1. Gladys Palmer, Labor Mobility in Six Cities, Chapters 5 and 6.

2. Gladys Palmer, Mobility and Economic Opportunity, Chapter 3, "Interpreting Patterns of Labor Mobility."

is most likely that these lifetime patterns in themselves are constantly changing as the entire social order changes. Therefore we hesitate to project these patterns far into the future - say a generation hence - for we have no assurance that the patterns observed among the present generation of men will necessarily apply with little change to their sons. We can proceed with reasonable confidence, however, in making projections a decade, or perhaps two decades, into the future.

That there may be considerable stability to these working life patterns over time is suggested in the last section of this chapter. It may be that future research would reveal that there is more stability than we anticipate. If such is the case, then it should be possible to make reasonable projections even further into the future than we have done. In the absence of a sufficient amount of such historical evidence, however, we are confining our actual projections to but one decade into the future.

In the following sections of this chapter we shall review the available information on: (1) average length of working life by occupation, (2) vertical movement up the occupational ladder in a span of three decades, (3) synthetic working life histories by occupation, as reconstructed from the data of the Six City Study, and (4) some observations on occupational change prior to 1930.

Average Length of Working Life

Before investigating the extent of mobility up the occupational ladder or before seeking out working life patterns, let us simply inquire as to the length of time which a man spends in his working career. Furthermore how do the various occupations compare with each other with regard to length of working life?

Approximate answers to these questions can be given on the basis of the data from our study on average age of entry into and retirement from the working force. Such computations were made as of the census years of 1930, 1940 and 1950. The difference between the two averages for any given occupation provides an estimate of the mean number of years spent in that occupation. This is of course a synthetic figure since, as we shall see, comparatively few men spend their entire working careers in the same occupation. This figure on "mean number of years" rather is a convenient way of summarizing the occupational differences in rates of new entries and retirements. For those men who do remain in the same major occupation group throughout their lives, it does provide an estimate of about how many years they would spend in the working force, given the entry and retirement patterns of a particular census year. For the entire working force without respect to occupation this figure is the mean length of working life, as of each census year.

For the entire working force the mean length of working life was about 46 years as of 1950 and 1940, and about 47 years as of 1930.[3] At all three periods the average age of retirement was about 65 years. Hence the decrease in length of working life was attributable to a later average age of entry as of 1940 and 1950. In 1930 the average age of entry was about 18 years whereas in 1940 and 1950 the average was about 19 years.

There was considerable variation in mean length of working life as among the various occupations. For example, "service workers" spent about 52 years in the working force whereas "professional, technical and kindred workers" spent only about 40 years as

---

3. Our mean length of working life for 1940, 46 years, may be compared with that presented by Harold Wool, "Tables of Working Life, Length of Working Life of Men," Bureau of Labor Statistics, Bulletin 1001, U. S. Department of Labor, July, 1950. As of 1940 Wool calculated the number of years which a 14-year-old boy could expect to be in the working force, as 46.6.

workers. These differences reflect different ages of entry and retirement. The ten major occupation groups can be summarized as follows (average age of entry and retirement as of 1950:

Occupation	Mean number years in working force	Average age of entry	Average age of retirement
Professional, technical and kindred workers	40 years	Above average	Below average
Managers, officials and proprietors, except farm	41 years	Above average	Below average
Craftsmen, foremen and kindred workers	44 years	Above average	Average
Operatives and kindred workers	45 years	Below average	Below average
Sales workers	47 years	Below average	Average
Clerical and kindred workers	47 years	Below average	Average
Farmers and farm managers	48 years	Above average	Above average
Laborers, except farm and mine	51 years	Below average	Above average
Farm laborers and foremen	52 years	Below average	Above average
Service workers	52 years	Below average	Above average

These differences as among the various occupations (in 1950) were largely similar to those observed in 1940 and 1930. In general the factors which contributed to determination of average age of entry or retirement from a specific occupation remained largely the same over the two decades.

In general men spend on the average few years in what may be termed the better jobs. The three with the shortest working life are those in which age of entry is older than the average for all occupations and for which greater training, education or experience are required. These are also the jobs which in general afford larger earnings. To get a more precise measurement, we can relate our previously used index of the quality of occupations (see p. 32) to the mean length of working life by occupation. This correlation is -.82. Clearly the men in the better jobs (as measured by earnings and education) spend a shorter period of their lives in the working force.

The Occupational Ladder

Our analysis thus far has ignored occupational mobility. Our calculations in the preceding section provided the mean length of working life if a man entered and remained until the time of his retirement in a given major occupation group. If he moved about among several occupations, then our preceding calculations provided no information about the number of years that he would actually spend in the working force and of course no information about his working life history, or pattern. Accordingly in this section let us investigate further the question of how much and what kinds of occupational mobility are actually experienced and relate them to the patterns of working life.

One way of pursuing this investigation is to follow through a given age cohort for as long a period as possible noting the changes which occurred. Our historical observations extend over only the two decades, 1930 to 1950. However, by adding on our 1960 projections, we can construct a 30-year span over which a given age cohort can be followed. Hence we can begin with a group of men aged 25 to 29 years in 1930 and inquire as to their occupational distribution at that date and compare it with their distribution in 1960 when they will be 55 to 59 years of age.[4] We can also study the cohort aged 30 to 34 years in 1930 and 60 to 64 years in 1960.

---

4. In order to simplify the presentation, we shall consider for 1960 only the B projections. Substantially the same conclusions would be reached if we had used the A projections (see page 9).

We can then group the occupations into a hierarchy such that changes as among occupations can be construed as changes in vertical mobility. By noting the changes which occur over the 30-year span, we can thus detect the extent to which men move up or down the occupational ladder.

More men move up the occupational ladder than move down. This is revealed by the fact that, among men aged 25 to 29 years in 1930, only about 13 percent were in the better paying jobs in nonagriculture (Table 12). Thirty years later, when these men are aged 55 to 59 years, about 24 percent of them are in these higher paying occupations. Conversely, in 1930, 38 percent had been in the poorer paying jobs whereas in 1960 only 31 percent of the cohort is in these inferior jobs in nonagriculture.

Within agriculture also there appears to be upward vertical mobility. Over the three decades the proportion of men who are farm laborers decreases much more than the proportion who are farmers and farm managers. This is in accordance with our previous analysis of net mobility in which we noted the very large net out movement from the group of farm laborers.

The same pattern of vertical mobility is noted for the age group 30 to 34 years in 1930 and 60 to 64 years in 1960. This cohort also succeeded in improving its occupational position in life. The improvement, however, is less pronounced than for the younger cohort.

Clearly very many men succeed in improving their occupational position during the course of their working careers. This is particularly the case during the first two or three decades of their working life. Some of them are able to maintain their better jobs and occupations until the time of their retirement or death. With advancing age, however, some are forced into inferior jobs, many of which are in the service industries.

During the three decades which we observed, there was a net shift from agriculture to nonagriculture. This is because occupational advancement tends to lie more in nonagriculture. Perhaps in earlier periods of American history, when economic opportunity may have been greater in agriculture, there may have been net movement from nonagriculture to agriculture; of that we do not know, however.

Most upward mobility seems to occur between about the ages of 25 to 45 years.[5] Some men of course continue to move up the occupational ladder beyond this age; others may remain in the same occupation but improve their job position via greater seniority rights, etc. On the other hand, some men may begin to move down the occupational ladder sometime around age 50 or thereabouts. We can generalize by saying that men tend to reach their highest position on the occupational ladder by about age 50. After that age a man is not likely to improve his position very much.

The exact age at which vertical mobility may slow down and perhaps halt, as well as the rapidity of vertical mobility at all ages, is in part a function of economic and labor market conditions. When there is a plentiful supply of better jobs, men continue to move upward even at the older ages; when there are few jobs, upward mobility is halted and downward mobility may set in. At the very oldest ages, many men are physically incapable of handling the better jobs, and if economic needs or other factors keep them in the working force, they accept whatever jobs they are capable of handling. Such jobs are necessarily those requiring lesser skill and physical strength and are generally at the lower end of the occupational scale.

5. See Chapter 5 on "Net Mobility," especially Chart 2.

TABLE 12

OCCUPATIONAL HIERARCHY OF MALE WORKING FORCE, 1930 AND 1960[1]
(Selected Age Cohorts)

1949 Occupational median income[2]	Cohort age 25 to 29 in 1930			Cohort age 30 to 34 in 1930		
	Percent in working force		Change	Percent in working force		Change
	1930	1960	1930 to 1960	1930	1960	1930 to 1960
Nonagricultural occupations	80.8	88.3	+ 7.5	81.5	87.7	+ 6.2
Better paying jobs (about $4000)[3]	12.7	23.5	+ 10.8	15.7	21.6	+ 5.9
Intermediate paying jobs (about $3000)[4]	30.2	33.7	+ 3.5	31.0	33.9	+ 2.9
Lower paying jobs ($2000 to $2600)[5]	37.9	31.1	- 6.8	34.8	32.2	- 2.6
Agricultural occupations	19.2	11.7	- 7.5	18.5	12.3	- 6.2
Farmers and farm managers[6]	10.5	9.7	- 0.8	12.8	10.1	- 2.7
Farm laborers and foremen[7]	8.7	2.0	- 6.7	5.7	2.2	- 3.5

1. 1960 distribution based on the B projection. See Appendix Table 1 and p. 9.
2. 1950 United States Census of Population, Bulletin P-C1, Table 129.
3. Professional, technical and kindred workers ($3758); managers, officials and proprietors ($3994).
4. Clerical and kindred workers ($3010); sales workers ($3125); craftsmen, foremen and kindred workers ($3125).
5. Operatives and kindred workers ($2607); service workers, except private household ($2195); laborers except farm and mine ($1961).
6. Farmers and farm managers ($1455).
7. Farm laborers and foremen ($863).

TABLE 13

MEN CLASSIFIED BY MAJOR OCCUPATION GROUP AT BEGINNING AND END OF WORKING CAREER*

Occupation at end of career	Total	Occupation at beginning of career						
		Professional, technical and kindred workers	Managers, officials and proprietors except farm	Clerical and kindred workers and sales workers	Craftsmen, foremen and kindred workers	Operatives and kindred workers	Service workers	Laborers except farm and mine
Total	10,000	548	371	1,854	1,254	3,092	675	2,206
Professional, technical and kindred workers	759	197	29	180	78	167	40	68
Managers, officials and proprietors, except farm	1,785	90	104	402	224	526	119	320
Clerical and kindred workers and sales workers	1,322	80	72	334	133	374	91	238
Craftsmen, foremen and kindred workers	2,651	78	76	413	425	869	150	640
Operatives and kindred workers	1,983	55	53	308	236	680	126	525
Service workers	994	37	25	145	109	315	111	252
Laborers except farm and mine	506	11	12	72	49	161	38	163

* Based on data from Six City Study; see text for further details.

Selected Working Life Histories

We just reviewed evidence showing that men work their way up the occupational ladder during the course of their working careers; indeed, more men rise than descend. Such vertical movement seems to be completed for the most part by about age 50. Since this analysis was based on census data, we had to infer our findings on the basis of net movements because the census data do not permit identifying the movements of individual workers. A movement up or down the occupational ladder - or a net gain or loss due to mobility (Chapter 5) - has told us nothing concerning the occupation from which the gain was made or the one to which it was lost; it has also told us nothing concerning mobility in the opposite direction which may have occurred simultaneously.

Fortunately additional information on the movements of individuals among the different occupations is available from the Six City Study.[6] In anticipation of the materials to be presented we shall simply say at this point only that this additional information confirms our previous findings with respect to vertical mobility. Furthermore these data permit us to draw much more precise pictures of the various working life patterns. We can find out, for example, just what happens to a group of boys who begin their working careers as operatives and in what occupations they finally end their working lives. This tells us more exactly how many move up the occupational ladder, how many move down, and how many remain put. As another example, we can determine where the men come from who end their careers as managers, officials and proprietors. From our previous analysis of new entries into the working force (Chapter 4), we know that very few boys and young men enter this occupation group at the beginning of their careers. On the contrary, this group grows through continuous net in-mobility (Chapter 5), but we have not been able to determine as yet from what occupations they come. It is this kind of question which we shall attempt to answer in this section.

---

6. The Six City Study provided information on the age and major occupation group of each man in both 1940 and 1950; hence it is possible to determine what types of occupational mobility occurred and at which ages. Thus, for example, we know how many men aged 15 to 24 in 1940, who were laborers then, rose to operatives in 1950 and how many who were operatives became laborers by 1950. Altogether the available information permits analysis of seven major occupation groups, all in nonagriculture. On the basis of these data we can construct synthetic working life patterns for nonagricultural occupations, assuming that the conditions of the 1940s were to apply to the entire working life.

Table 13 in which the results are presented was constructed as follows. We assume that 1000 boys between the ages of 15 and 24 years have entered each of the seven occupation groups. Using the data from the Six City Study on actual interchange among the occupations, by age, we trace the movements of these boys about from occupation to occupation and from one decade to the next until they have reached the age group of 55 to 64 years. In making these computations, we assume that the occupational changes by age observed in the 1940s will apply to their entire working lives. The final table thus derived was then weighted by the actual distribution of new entries as of 1940. Hence Table 13 shows the occupations in which 10,000 men begin and end their working careers. Obviously under economic and labor market conditions different from those of the 1940s somewhat different career patterns would have emerged. Until the Six City Study or a similar one is repeated, however, no further data will be available.

Professional, technical and kindred workers. Of 1000 young men who enter this occupation and survive 40 years, about one third will have remained in this major group. Perhaps another one third will have become either managers, officials or proprietors or clerical and sales workers. Movement into the managerial group may not be vertical mobility since average earnings and status seem to be about the same. Movement into the clerical and sales groups in general may be construed as downward mobility, since these latter jobs provide lower average earnings (see Table 12) and seem to have lower social status. However, many of these so-called "lower" white collar jobs are very remunerative and carry considerable status. For example, does a prosperous automobile salesman necessarily have lower status than an elementary school teacher? The former certainly earns more than the latter. In short it is difficult to determine how much downward mobility there is from the professional to the "lower" white collar ranks.

About one third of these neophyte professionals will end their working careers as manual workers in nonagriculture; perhaps one sixth will be skilled craftsmen and one sixth will end as operatives, service workers, and some even as common laborers (Table 13). Despite the fact that some of the manual occupations provide larger earnings than do some of the professional jobs, most of this movement can be characterized as downward mobility.

Since there is considerable mobility into this occupation, let us examine the men in it at the end of their career and inquire regarding the occupations in which they first entered the working force. About one quarter of the men at the end of their working career had begun as professionals. About one quarter worked their way into it from clerical and sales positions, and perhaps one quarter had begun as operatives. About one in ten of the professionals had begun as laborers.

Managers, officials and proprietors, except farm. Of 1000 young men who enter this occupation prior to age 25, not many more than one quarter will remain in it to the end of their working careers. About one fifth will become clerical and sales workers, and but a few will enter the professions. Almost half will become manual workers almost equally divided between craftsmen and other manual jobs.

As noted previously, this occupation grows mainly through net in-mobility, particularly at the older ages, rather than as a result of youths beginning their working careers in it. Accordingly it is relevant to ask from what occupations have these managers and officials come. Of all men in this occupation at the end of their working careers, it would appear that only about one third began their working lives as white collar workers. About one in ten began as a craftsman, three in ten as operatives, and two in ten as laborers. Of all these men only one in twenty had started his career in this occupation group. This is in marked contrast to the professional workers, among whom about one in four had begun his career as a professional worker (Table 13).

Clerical and sales workers. Young men tend to enter these occupations in rather large numbers and subsequently move to other occupations. Of the youths in these jobs at the beginning of their work careers, about one fifth remain in them to the end of their careers. About one fifth shift to the group of "managers, officials and proprietors, except farm" and perhaps one tenth to the professional group. About one tenth move to the group of "craftsmen, foremen and kindred workers" and about two fifths to other manual occupations.

In terms of the occupational ladder we may conclude that about three in ten end about where they began, i.e., in the clerical and sales or craftsmen's jobs, at about the middle of the occupational ladder. Another three in ten end near the top of the

7. Jaffe and Stewart, Manpower, p. 389.

ladder, i.e., in the professional and managerial groups. And four in ten move down the ladder into the lower manual jobs.

Large numbers of men who began working as operatives and laborers subsequently rise to become clerical and sales workers. At the end of their working life we find that, of all clerical and sales workers, about three in ten had begun as operatives and two in ten as laborers.

Summary of the white collar occupations. In general a larger proportion of those who begin their working careers in higher status occupations remains in them for the duration of their working lives. Of those who start at the lower levels of the white collar scale, namely the clerical and sales workers, large numbers work their way into the better white collar jobs, and a large number become craftsmen.

If we consider movement from white collar jobs into those of operatives, service workers and laborers as downward mobility, then we must conclude that only about one fourth of the white collar workers experience downward occupational mobility. More men end their working careers in white collar occupations than begin in such occupations. For every 100 men who begin in these occupations and survive to the end of their working lives, there will be about 140 men in white collar occupations. In what occupations did these 140 men begin working? About four in ten had begun as white collar workers. About one in ten had begun as a craftsman, and five in ten had begun in other manual work.

Vertical occupational mobility can be summarized as follows: if movement from white collar to operatives, service workers and laborers be considered as downward mobility, then for every 100 men who so move down the occupational scale, almost 300 move up during the course of a lifetime.

Craftsmen, foremen and kindred workers. Of 1000 youths under age 25 in this occupation about one third will remain in it to the end of their working lives. Another one third will enter white collar occupations, and another one third will move into the lower status and lower pay manual jobs of operatives, service workers and laborers.

This occupation experiences considerable in-mobility; for every 100 men who begin their careers as craftsmen, about 200 end their working careers as such skilled workers. From what occupations does the influx come? About one third of the craftsmen begin working as operatives and about one quarter as laborers. Only about two in ten begin as white collar workers.

Operatives and kindred workers. Youths enter this occupation in large numbers because relatively little skill is required, and hence it is fairly easy to obtain such jobs (assuming that there are jobs available). Thereafter there is considerably more out-mobility than in-mobility so that at the end of their working careers there are far fewer men in this occupation than started. For every 100 men who begin their careers in this occupation, only about 60 end their careers as operatives. When they move out of this occupation, where do they go?

About one third enter the white collar occupations, mostly into the managerial, clerical and sales jobs; only a small proportion enters the professions. About three in ten become craftsmen, and relatively few enter the service occupations or become laborers. About two men in ten remain operatives for their entire working lives.

The men who begin working in other occupations and end as operatives come from all occupations. About two in ten come from white collar jobs, one in ten from craftsmen, and one quarter from laborers. In short most boys who begin as operatives work their way into better jobs. The jobs which they vacate are filled largely by new entries into the working force and by movement of laborers upwards into better jobs. The downward movement of white collar workers and craftsmen is relatively small.

Service workers. Comparatively few youths begin their working careers in this occupation. Of those who do, about four in ten work their way up into white collar jobs and two in ten become craftsmen. The other four in ten remain service workers or become operatives, and only a few become laborers. In short perhaps six in ten experience upward mobility, a few downward mobility and the others remain at about the same station throughout life.

More men end their careers as service workers than begin as such. For every 100 who begin in this occupation about 150 end in it. We have already noted that most of those who begin their work careers in this occupation subsequently leave it. From what occupations then do the men come who end their careers as service workers? About one fifth had been white collar workers and one tenth craftsmen; the majority had been operatives and laborers.

Laborers except farm and mine. As is the case with operatives, large numbers of youths enter this occupation because it is so easy to do so, no training being required. Very few remain in it, however, for the course of their lifetime. About three in ten work their way up to white collar jobs and an equal number to craftsmen jobs. Almost one quarter become operatives and one tenth service workers.

As these men leave the laborer occupation group, they are largely replaced by new entries into the working force. This can be seen in the fact that for every 100 men who begin working as laborers only about 25 end their working lifetime in such jobs. A few men who begin working in other occupations drift down to the status of laborer. For the most part, however, such jobs which the economy may require are filled by the newcomers to the working force.

Summary of the manual occupations. As is the case with the white collar occupations, a larger proportion of those who begin their working careers in higher status manual occupations remains in them for the duration of their working lives. Of those who begin in the lower status occupations, particularly operatives and laborers, the majority shift to white collar and skilled occupations. Comparatively few men move downward to these lower status occupations, however; to the extent that the economy needs to fill these jobs, they tend to be filled by new entries into the working force.

We can consider movement of craftsmen into operatives, service workers and laborers as downward mobility; perhaps one third of those who begin as craftsmen experience such downward mobility. Whether movement into all white collar jobs should be considered as upward mobility is not clear. Movement into the professions and managerial ranks is definitely upward mobility, but movement into the clerical and sales ranks is not necessarily so. In general craftsmen earn about the same amount as do clerical and sales workers, and insofar as public opinion is concerned, both have about the same status, namely, below professional and managerial workers and above operatives and laborers.

Since the remaining manual jobs (other than craftsmen) are being considered as lower status, then any movement out of them is necessarily upward mobility. Taking these three lower status occupations together, it would appear that only four in ten of the men who enter them remain in them; the other six move up the occupational ladder. Even this figure minimizes the amount of upward mobility, however, because it fails to take into consideration the preponderance of upward movement from laborer to operative.

Summary of all occupations. (1) Only about one man in five remains in the same major occupation group for his entire working life. The other four men move about from occupation to occupation such that their final occupation is in a quite different category from the one in which they began working.

(2) How much shifting is there between white collar and manual occupations? Of those men who begin working in a white collar job, a little over half end their careers in a white collar occupation. Of those who begin in a manual occupation, about two thirds end in a manual job. In short there is not complete mobility between white collar and manual occupations; men tend to end their working lives in that major type of occupation in which they began.[8]

(3) We should like to be able to stratify precisely these seven major occupation groups in terms of status, both social and economic. Unfortunately this cannot be done with any great degree of accuracy; therefore, it is difficult to measure the amount of vertical mobility, both upward and downward. The conclusions which seem to derive from our analysis are as follows:

(a) In general those who begin their working careers near the top of the occupational order tend to remain there. Furthermore larger proportions of those who begin in such jobs remain in the same major occupation group in which they begin for their entire working lives than is the case among workers who start at the bottom of the occupational ladder.

(b) Of those who begin near the bottom of the occupational ladder, more move upward than downward; furthermore, more of them move upward than do men who begin toward the center of the occupational ladder.

(c) However, those who begin near the bottom of the occupational ladder and move upward do not move quite as far upward as those who begin at about the center. In short comparatively fewer men who begin as lower white collar or craftsmen will move up the occupational ladder; those who do, however, will move into the top occupations, the professions and managerial groups. On the other hand, more men who begin as operatives and laborers will move upward, but comparatively few of them will reach the top occupations.

Occupational Mobility Prior to 1930

Our study did not attempt to measure the extent of occupational mobility prior to 1930. However, there is good reason to believe that there must have been very considerable amounts of such mobility in earlier decades. We cannot say whether there was more or less in the period of say, 1890 to 1930, than there is expected to be in the period of 1930 to 1960; we can say, however, that there was a great deal of such mobility in the earlier period. The evidence for this comes from Edward's[9] social-economic groupings of native white males in the United States in 1930. If we compare the percentage distributions of the social-economic groupings for men aged 20 to 24 years with those aged 60 to 64 years, we conclude that most likely there had been a great deal of mobility. The data are as follows:

---

8. See also Gladys Palmer, Labor Mobility in Six Cities, p. 93. See also Chapter 6 of Palmer's volume in which she emphasizes that there are limits to the amount of interchange which is possible among occupations.

9. Alba M. Edwards, A Social-Economic Grouping of the Gainful Workers of the United States, U. S. Bureau of the Census, Washington, 1938, Table 10.

| | Age in 1930 | | Difference |
	20-24 years	60-64 years	
Nonagriculture			
Professional persons	3.8	4.6	+ 0.8
Proprietors, managers and officials			
Wholesale and retail dealers	1.9	5.9	+ 4.0
Other proprietors, etc.	1.4	7.0	+ 5.6
Clerks and kindred workers	18.7	10.8	- 7.9
Skilled workers and foremen	13.3	16.8	+ 3.5
Semi-skilled workers	19.8	8.5	- 11.3
Unskilled workers			
Factory and other laborers	17.0	10.7	- 6.3
Servant classes	1.3	2.1	+ 0.8
Agriculture			
Farmers	6.5	28.3	+ 21.8
Farm laborers	16.4	5.3	- 11.1
Total	100.0	100.0	-

Inspection of these data further suggests that the patterns of mobility must have been fairly similar prior to 1930 with those subsequent to 1930 which we reported in our study. Note that with advancing age there is an increase in the proportions in the professional, managerial and proprietor groups, and in the skilled workers. Simultaneously there are decreases among the clerks, semi-skilled workers (equivalent to operatives), and among the laborers, both in agriculture and nonagriculture. Among Edwards' "servant classes" (approximately comparable to our "service workers") there was a small increase with advancing age.

The analysis would be more precise if we could compare a given cohort of men over time. It would have been preferable if we could have compared the social-economic distribution of native white males aged 20 to 24 in 1890 with that of the same cohort 40 years later, in 1930, when they were aged 60 to 64. Edwards did not prepare the data for such an analysis, however, and our study could not undertake to do so. Hence we are forced to infer previous trends by comparing, as of one date, the two age groups representing approximately the beginning and end of the working life, as we just did. Despite the inadequacies in this type of approach, the differences are great and in much the same direction as those we uncovered subsequent to 1930; we can only conclude that patterns of working life observed as of about the mid-twentieth century are quite similar to those as of the beginning of the twentieth century.

Summary

The United States was and still is the land of opportunity. Most men move about from one job to another during the course of their working lives so that they end in occupations often very different from those in which they began. In this process they succeed in climbing the occupational ladder so that very many reach jobs considerably above those in which they began their working careers. The majority of men improve both their economic and status positions.

This upward mobility is influenced by several factors. One is the normal upward movement from "apprentice to craftsman" found in many societies, even those with rather rigid class lines. Many occupations have to be learned, and the learner is in a lower position until he has mastered the occupation and risen to the status of craftsman. This applies not only to the traditional manual craftsman occupations, but to managerial, and even many professional occupations. Another factor is the availability of jobs; if the labor demand schedule so changes that there is a great increase in the demand for workers in the better jobs - those near the top of the occupational scale - then this can permit upward mobility.[10] A third factor is the phase of the business cycle; during periods of economic prosperity upward mobility is enhanced, and during periods of economic depression, retarded.

Historically in the United States all three of these influences have been and still are operative. Youths cannot enter many of the occupations at the very top of the ladder until they have served an apprenticeship of some sort. The factory owner's son who begins working on the assembly line in order to learn all about the enterprise so that he will be able to operate it efficiently still exists.

With reference to the changes in the economy's demand for labor, it is clear that there has been a long-time increased demand for workers in the higher occupations. In the last several decades many men have moved up the occupational ladder if for no other reason than that the economy needed more workers in these jobs. From the viewpoint of the individual's position in life, however, it may make little difference whether he obtains a better job because of sheer personal brilliance or because such a job was available for the mere asking; in either event he moves into a job higher on the occupational ladder.

With respect to the influence of the phase of the business cycle, this is apt to be a temporary matter. A working lifetime, stretching over 40 or 50 years as it does, embraces both periods of prosperity and depression so that sometime during the course of their working lives some opportunity for occupational advancement is presented to most men. They live through several periods of prosperity, in each of which some opportunity for upward mobility is presented, albeit in the intervening depression periods they are sore pressed to remain at whatever level they find themselves.

Whether the opportunities were greater in the nineteenth century or are greater in the twentieth we do not know; the available evidence is insufficient to determine this point. It may be that the settling of the West in the nineteenth century provided the opportunities. On the other hand, it may be that the growth of the electronics and similar industries in the mid-twentieth century is providing the better opportunities. We do not know, and the answer probably does not matter too much anyhow. It is sufficient to say that considerable upward mobility exists at present.

Although every man has the opportunity to climb the occupational ladder, it seems that he who starts closer to the top is quite likely to remain there. Those boys who begin working in the better jobs are very likely to end their working careers in the better jobs.

Most of those boys who begin working at the lower end of the occupational ladder will work their way up, but only part way up. Comparatively few of them will reach the top of the ladder. This may be a reflection, in part, of the fact that these boys receive less formal education than do the boys who begin in the better jobs. And perhpas this initial handicap can never be quite overcome by the majority.

There are many other impediments to upward mobility of course; lack of sufficient education is but one of them. Our job, however, called for devising models which would permit making projections to 1960 of the occupational distribution of American males; it did not call for analyzing the question of vertical mobility in American society. And on this note we shall end.

---

10. For a discussion of this point see Natalie Rogoff, <u>Recent Trends in Occupational Mobility</u>, The Free Press, Glenco, Illinois, 1953, Chapter II.

CHAPTER 8
INTRODUCTION

Resume of the Methodological Problems

Objectives. This study was conceived initially as an exploratory, methodological study. Its general objective was to develop models for making projections of the occupational distribution of a country's working force from one census period to the next, models which, taking into account some of the most important components of occupational change, would have a precision and reliability not generally characteristic of sheer mathematical extrapolations of gross figures. It was also hoped that an exploratory study of this type could serve the useful purpose of making clear the essential data requirements necessary for the workability of such a model.

In developing these models, it became necessary also to test them with data to determine their practicality. As a result, cohort and component analyses were made of the patterns of occupational change of the experienced civilian male working force in the United States by major occupation group and by age between 1930 and 1940 and between 1940 and 1950. These were then followed with projections of the numbers of males in each occupation group in 1960. These calculations were presented in Table 1. The purpose of this Methodology Section is to describe the details and the implications of the models and to explain how they were employed to make the projections to 1960.

Description of universe studied. The universe whose occupational distribution was projected to 1960 is the total United States experienced civilian male working force, aged 15 to 74 years. This universe comprises the employed and also the unemployed except those who had never worked before and therefore did not in general have an occupation.

The military were excluded because the civilian working force is of much greater interest for many practical purposes, as well as being more amenable to projection. After all, the size, occupational and age structure of the military is largely a function of government decision rather than the resultant of the interplay of economic and social factors. Hence the size and characteristics of the military can be much more variable than the size of the civilian working force.

The scope was restricted to males because our models would not be applicable to females without considerable modifications made necessary because of the variable pattern of female working force participation. It is well known that many more women than men enter, withdraw, and re-enter the working force during the course of their lifetime.

Males 75 years of age and over - never constituting as much as one percent of the male working force and therefore not being an important factor in its occupational structure - were excluded mainly because our models could not be applied to them without data on their occupational distribution by five, or at least ten, year age grouping, and census tabulations do not provide this information. While this information could have been estimated by one device or another, it was felt that the time consumed in this way would not be commensurate with its substantive importance.

Major methodological problems. The main procedural steps taken in order to achieve the final 1960 projections may be outlined as follows:

1. For the intercensal period 1930 to 1940 separate balancing equations were employed for each occupation, and within each occupation, for each five-year age cohort. In the case of each balancing equation, data were either obtained or approximated for five of the six terms:

O_1 - number in occupation and age cohort in 1930
O_2 - number in occupation and age cohort in 1940
D - deaths in occupation and age cohort from 1930 to 1940
NE - new entries in occupation and age cohort from 1930 to 1940
R - retirements in occupation and age cohort from 1930 to 1940

Net mobility (NM) in each occupation for each age cohort was then derived residually as that amount which was necessary in order for the right-hand side of the balancing equation to be equal to the left-hand side:

$$O_2 = O_1 - D + NE - R \pm NM$$

The same procedure was followed for the intercensal period 1940 to 1950.

2. Intercensal new entry rates, retirement rates and net mobility rates were computed for both decades by occupation and by five-year age cohort. Using these rates as well as census survival rates computed from the United States Census Bureau's population projections for 1960, two different sets of 1960 working force projections (one set under the assumption that new entry, retirement and net mobility rates for the period 1950 to 1960 would be the same as in 1930 to 1940, i.e., a period of depression; and the other set assuming that they would be the same as in 1940 to 1950, i.e., a period of economic prosperity) were obtained by completely filling in the right-hand side of the balancing equations for the intercensal period 1950 to 1960.

Summing the right-hand side of each balancing equation in accordance with the specific procedures detailed in the following chapters yielded two sets of estimates of the numbers in each occupation by five-year age cohorts, i.e., two sets of estimates of the occupational distribution of the experienced civilian male working force by age for 1960. The totals for all age groups combined were shown in Table 1. It will be recalled that Table 1 also included two sets of projections in which additional allowances were made for the military. As will be described in more detail following, these projections - A' and B' - were obtained by subtracting off from the previous summations the hypothesized allowance for the military.

The major methodological problems encountered were mostly involved in assigning numerical values to the terms of the balancing equations for the intercensal periods 1930 to 1940 and 1940 to 1950:

a. Numerical data by occupation and by five-year age group (O_1 and O_2) were obtained from the 1930, 1940 and 1950 censuses. The major problem here was the occupational comparability of the three censuses. However, other comparability questions questions also had to be faced. How these problems of comparability were handled is discussed in Chapter 9.

b. Intercensal data on deaths (D) among the working force by occupation and by age were not available and therefore had to be estimated. The estimating procedure adopted and the reasons for adopting it are discussed in Chapter 10, on Census Survival Rates.

c. Methods also had to be developed for estimating intercensal new entries (NE in the balancing equation) and retirements (R) by occupation and age. These methods, which are very similar, are elaborated upon in Chapter 11 on New Entries and Chapter 12 on Retirements.

d. As already stated, net mobility (NM) estimates by occupation and age were obtained residually after having filled in all other terms of each balancing equation. Problems encountered in the course of arriving at these estimates and their significance for the concept of net mobility as herein used are discussed in Chapter 13 on Net Mobility.

e.   Chapter 14 treats certain problems of adjustment that had to be made before all the balancing equations for each of the two decades could be tabulated in final form, thus summarizing the patterns of occupational change.

f.   In Chapter 15 the methodological aspects of the 1960 working force projections are discussed in detail.

Resulting By-Product Statistics

The major aim of the investigation was to provide the series of projections for 1960. In implementing the models, however, a number of additional statistics resulted - statistical tables upon which the 1960 projections are based. These additional, or by-product, statistics not only are necessary parts of the models but have considerable interest in themselves, and are accordingly being listed here.

a.   The occupational structures of the experienced civilian male working force in 1930 and 1940 by five-year age groups have been re-tabulated and made occupationally comparable with the 1950 occupational groupings.

b.   New entries and retirements during the census years 1930, 1940 and 1950 by occupation and age have been calculated both by volume and by rates.

c.   For each of the past two decades the components of change for each five-year age cohort in each major occupation group have been summarized in balancing equation form. A similar tabulation has been made for each major occupation group showing components of change by age.

d.   Intercensal new entry, retirement and net mobility volume and rates for the 1930s and the 1940s.

Primary Sources of Data

1.   _1930 census_

Fifteenth Census of the United States: 1930, Population, Volume V, General Report on Occupations

Table 6 - Gainful Workers 10 Years Old and Over, by Occupation, Age, and Sex, pp. 118-137. (Gainful workers classified by industry and then by occupation within industry. Five-year age groupings except for 10 to 17, 18 and 19, 75 and over, and age unknown. Complete enumeration.)

Table 10 - Gainfully Occupied Children 10 to 17 Years Old, by Occupation, Sex, and Age, pp. 352-57. (10 to 17-year olds tabulated 10 to 13 and then by single year of age for 14 to 17; occupations listed as in Table 6 above. Complete enumeration.)

Table 2 - Persons 10 Years Old and Over in Each Industry or Service Group, by Occupation, Sex, Color, Nativity and Age, pp. 412-587. (Provides same information as Table 6 above with fewer age groupings, but with more detailed classification of industries and of occupations within industries. Complete enumeration.)

2.   _1940 census_

Sixteenth Census of the United States, 1940, Population, The Labor Force, (Sample Statistics), Occupational Characteristics

Table 1 - Age of Employed Persons (Except on Public Emergency Work) and of Experienced Workers Seeking Work, by Occupation and Sex, . . . pp. 11-14. (Experienced workers classified by major occupation group and subgroups; age by five-year groups except for 14 and 15, 16 and 17, 18 and 19, and 65 and over. 5 percent sample.)

Volume III, The Labor Force, Part I: United Summary

Table 65 - Age of Employed Persons (Except on Public Emergency Work) and of Experienced Workers Seeking Work, by Occupation and Sex, . . . pp. 98-101. (Same occupational classification as Table 1 above, but with different age groups; age 65 and over in Table 1 subdivided into 65 to 74 and 75 and over. Complete enumeration.)

Table 80 - pp. 197-220

Characteristics of the Population, United States Summary

Table 7 - Age, by Race and Sex, for the United States, Urban and Rural: 1940 and 1930, pp. 16-20. (Five-year age groups except for 75 and over; urban, rural-non-farm and rural-farm; native white, foreign-born white, Negro, and other races; 1930 and 1940. Complete enumeration.)

Special tabulation for male emergency workers by age and major group of usual occupation.

3. 1950 census

Pre-publication Tabulation

Age of the Experienced Civilian Labor Force by Detailed Occupation, for the United States: 1950. (Experienced civilian workers classified by major occupation group and sub-groups; age by five-year groups except 14 and 15, 16 and 17, 18 and 19, and 75 and over. 3-1/3 percent sample.)

1950 United States Census of Population, U. S. Summary, General Characteristics, P-B1

Table 38 - Age by Color and Sex for the United States, Urban and Rural: 1950 and 1940. (Age by five-year groups except 75 to 84 and 85 and over; age under 20 also given in more detail. Complete enumeration.)

CHAPTER 9
COMPARABILITY OF DATA

Most of the difficulties encountered in the application of the models were difficulties in connection with data; inadequate data, inaccurate data or incomparable data.

Sometimes the data were inadequate because they had not been tabulated in sufficient detail (for example, working force data by single year of age were seldom available and occasionally even five-year age groupings were not always to be had) and sometimes necessary tabulations had not been made at all (for example, working force by nativity in order to eliminate the effect of international migration). Data difficulties of this nature will present themselves throughout this section on methodology and will be taken up separately in the appropriate context as the occasion arises.

Inaccurate data resulted in no great damage wherever the inaccuracy was consistent among units being analyzed in relation to one another. For example, an under-enumeration of working force participants that is proportionately constant among all age groups and occupations at all censuses will not vitiate the resulting analyses. When, however, the inaccuracy is not consistent among units under analysis (for example, under-enumeration of working force participants of persons under 20 but not for age groups 20 and over), then the units are not strictly comparable. Hence data inaccuracy difficulties in this study were all reducible to special cases of incomparability, the subject matter of this chapter.

Three main kinds of data incomparability had to be coped with: (a) incomparability of occupational categorization, (b) incomparability with respect to coverage, and (c) incomparability of age data due to inaccurate age-reporting or enumeration.

Occupational Comparability

The first major problem that had to be resolved was that of making the 1930 and 1940 occupational classifications comparable to that of the 1950 census. The 1930 and 1940 data on occupation by age had to be re-tabulated in accordance with the 1950 occupational classification. Three special types of difficulties had to be surmounted:

1. The grouping of detailed occupations into major occupational categories by the 1950 Census of Population Index of Occupations and Industries was different in some respects from the grouping used in 1940. For example, the occupation "linemen and servicemen, telegraph, telephone and power" was classified as "craftsmen, foremen and kindred workers" in 1950; in 1940 it had been listed as "operatives and kindred workers." Incomparabilities of this type, as long as separately listed in the original census tabulation, could be adjusted easily enough simply by reassigning these occupations to the major occupational group in which the occupation had been classified in 1950.

2. Sometimes two or more detailed occupations, which belonged to different major occupational categories according to the 1950 index, had been listed together in either or both of the previous censuses. In the 1930 census "laborers, porters and helpers in stores" had all been tabulated together; in subsequent censuses "porters" were classified as "service workers," while "laborers and helpers in stores" were located in "laborer except farm and mine." Similarly, in the 1940 census, "bookkeepers, accountants and cashiers" were all listed together under "clerical workers"; the 1950 classification, on the other hand, had changed "accountants" over to "professional, technical and kindred workers." Incomparabilities of this type were adjusted in accordance with recommendations made by David L. Kaplan, Chief, Occupation and Industry Statistics Unit of the U. S. Census Bureau, and by members of his staff.

3. The 1930 occupation data had been tabulated on an entirely different basis from that employed in 1940 and 1950; instead of a tabulation by major occupational categories within each of which detailed occupations were itemized, the 1930 census grouped the detailed occupations under major industrial categories. In what proved to be a

relatively large-scale clerical operation, we recoded according to the 1950 index every line of Table 6 of Volume V of the 1930 census, consulting Table 2 at the back of the volume wherever appropriate. Invaluable assistance was again provided by the Census Bureau which reviewed our coding of each listing, giving special attention to doubtful items and to listings that brought together on the same line several detailed occupations which had been classified into different major occupational groupings by the 1950 index.

In addition to these difficulties, removing the military from the labor force tabulations of the 1940 census was complicated by virtue of the fact that an estimated 54 or 55 thousand military (commissioned officers, enlisted men with a military occupational specialty of professional worker, clerical worker or craftsman) were not tabulated as military and therefore were not identifiable as such. The necessary adjustment was made in accordance with the judgment of the Census Bureau.

Comparability With Respect to Coverage

1. The most serious coverage incomparability among the three censuses derives from the difference between the gainfully occupied and the labor force criteria of working force participation. The gainful worker approach - based essentially on whether or not a person had an occupation at which he is usually engaged for pay or profit - employed by the 1930 census defines more persons as being in the working force (especially marginal workers, the youngest and the oldest among the males) than the labor force technique - whether or not a person worked or looked for work during the census week - adopted by the 1940 and the 1950 censuses. As a consequence, working participation rates show up as being higher in 1930 than in 1940 or 1950 for all age groups.

No factual information was available which would have permitted defensible adjustments to the 1930 data. Before such adjustments could have been made, coverage differences with respect to occupation by age between the two different methods of measuring working force participation would have to be known. All that could be done therefore was to take cognizance of the discrepancy and of its possible implications in the course of analyzing and interpreting the data. In particular, some allowance for incomparability must be made when interpreting the estimated volume of new entries and retirements during the 1930s. Estimates of intercensal retirements in this decade are somewhat too high since men who would have been counted as retired by the current working force definition of participation were included in the working force in 1930. Because of the incomparability some men get retired who already were retired, i.e., would have been counted as retired in 1930 if the labor force definition of participation had been used.

Conversely estimates of intercensal new entries during the 1930s are somewhat too low since the 1930 census counted as already having entered the working force some young men who by the criteria of the working force procedures had not yet in fact entered.

2. It should be noted also that the gainfully occupied and the working force techniques are not strictly comparable on the occupational level. With the working force approach occupation means current occupation (or last occupation in the case of the unemployed) instead of usual occupation as in the case of the gainful worker. However, for the overwhelming majority of the working force current and usual occupation are identical.[1]

---

1. Information permitting comparison of the current and usual occupation for men is available from the 1940 census. Among employed men, 92.9 percent reported current and usual occupation in the same major occupation group; among the experienced seeking work, 89.8 percent reported the same major occupation group. See Population, the Labor Force, Usual Occupation, Sixteenth Census of the United States, 1940, Table II, p. 3.

3. To obtain the 1940 experienced civilian male labor force, it was necessary to combine separate tabulations of the employed, the unemployed seeking work, and public emergency workers. The 2,072,094 emergency workers presented somewhat of a special problem because of "the restricted character of emergency-work projects, which frequently utilized large numbers of men as laborers in various types of unskilled work" so that "the usual occupation of many emergency workers were undoubtedly different from the emergency occupations to which they were assigned.[2] Also "many emergency workers probably reported their usual or last nonemergency job instead of the emergency occupation to which they were assigned." Accordingly it was deemed advisable to classify these emergency workers by their usual occupation. But for all the rest of the male working force in 1940, 94.7% of the total, current occupation was utilized.

In the case of the 1950 census no such question arose; occupation here refers only to current occupation.

4. Another factor preventing perfect comparability between the 1940 and 1950 censuses are the revisions made in the schedule of questions used by the enumerators. The experience of the Current Population Survey shows that these revisions made in July, 1945, added 1.5 millions to the ranks of the civilian employed.[3] It should be added that most of these newly-found workers were women. The consequences of these revisions upon the male working force - which is our frame of reference - therefore are probably not very great. In any event no defensible adjustment could be made for the inconsistency in method of enumeration between the two censuses.

5. Within the 1950 census itself a problem arose in the form of an inconsistency between data tabulated on the basis of a complete enumeration of the population and data based on the 20 percent sample. Table 97 of Bulletin P-C1 (the 20 percent sample) showed 633,000 fewer males in the population than Table 38 of P-B1 (the complete enumeration). Moreover the difference between the two series is not evenly distributed by age and apparently also by such other important characteristics as residence and color; the sample tabulations contain more males under 20 and fewer males over 20 than the tabulations based on complete enumeration. There is good reason to suspect that the sampling bias is spread differentially by occupation as well. Since 1950 working force data used in this study are based on a 3-1/3 percent sample, a sub-sample of the 20 percent sample, our data are obviously affected by this bias in the 20 percent sample tabulations. No factual basis existed for adjusting differential occupational bias; the most that could be done was to increase the labor force total within each age group (and each occupation in the age group) by an amount proportionate to the difference between the PB and PC data in total male population for the given age group. In this way the bias by age was eliminated; to what extent bias by working force participation and by occupation was thereby also eliminated cannot be determined without intensive research into the nature of such bias - intensive research far beyond the scope of this study.

6. The enumeration bias discussed above is only one of several reasons leading one to believe that the quality of enumeration in 1950 was inferior to the standards adhered to in the 1940 census. The general lower working force participation rates at almost all age levels in 1950 is partial evidence that marginal workers, whose participation in the working force would have been noted by a more careful enumeration, were actually missed. Further confirmation is found in an analysis of detailed occupations where a large use of NEC (Not Elsewhere Classified) may be observed in the 1950 data.

---

2. <u>Sixteenth Census of the United States: 1940, Population</u>, Vol. III, The Labor Force, Part 1, p. 10.

3. U. S. Bureau of the Census, "The Labor Force," MRLF - No. 39, September 20, 1945.

7. A much less serious difference was also found between the complete enumeration tabulations of the labor force in the 1940 census (Table 65 of Vol. III, Part 1) and the tabulations based on a 5 percent sample (Table 1 of Population, The Labor Force (Sample Statistics), Occupational Characteristics). In this instance the labor force size based on sample data was some 107,000 larger than when complete enumeration data were used.

In this study the 5 percent sample data were used because of the more detailed age classification provided. However, the complete enumeration data had to be used in the case of those over 65 where the age detail was better than in the sample data. Internal consistency was achieved by adjusting the numbers of labor force males 65 and over in the complete enumeration data to the level of the 5 percent sample tabulations.

8. Incomparability between the Current Population Surveys and the censuses prevented use of CPS figures for the estimates of occupational trends since the 1950 census. For one thing the employed experienced civilian male labor force, as estimated by the CPS in April, 1950, was almost one million higher than the 1950 census count[4] and what is much more troublesome, this difference is far from being distributed proportionately among the occupational groups. Although the CPS estimate was higher in total, five of the ten major occupations were higher according to the census figures. Hence CPS and census data for some of the remaining occupations were so far out of line as to appear completely unrelated to each other. There were 1,097,000 more "managers, proprietors and officials," for example, according to the CPS estimate – a difference almost three times as large as the sampling variability. Therefore it was felt that an analysis of occupational changes shown by the CPS figures between April, 1950, and April, 1953, would be of little help in estimating changes subsequent to 1950 on a basis comparable to the 1950 census data.

Comparability of Age Reporting

Census age data are in general subject to two different kinds of errors: differential completeness of enumeration by age and misreporting of age by those enumerated. A brief discussion of these kinds of errors in the 1940 and 1950 censuses may be found in 1940 Census of Population, Vol. IV, Characteristics by Age, Part 1, page 3, and 1950 Census of Population, P-C1, page XIII. Their relevance for the application of our model was felt in two different ways:

1. Accurate five-year age cohort analysis is presented if persons alive at two successive censuses are either not enumerated at both censuses or are not reported in the same cohort (i.e., the same age group aged by ten years) at each census. In 1940 and 1950, possibly because of the Old Age and Survivors Insurance legislation, there appeared a deficit of persons relative to what might be expected in the age range 55 to 64; and correspondingly, the numbers reported as 65 and over were unexpectedly large. Incomparabilities occur in other cohorts also. For instance, "males between the ages of 18 and 34 also appear to have been relatively underenumerated" in 1950 (P-C1, page XIII). Age cohort incomparability, as will be brought out more clearly in subsequent chapters, necessitated adjustments in our techniques for estimating the components of occupational change from one decade to the next.

2. Statistics for single years of age are not smooth partly because of irregularities in the annual numbers of births and partly because of a tendency towards the

---

4. 41,492,000 according to Current Population Reports Labor Force, Series P-54, No. 94, page 11, and 40,519,462 according to page 1-101 of Vol. P-B1 of the 1950 United States of Population.

over-reporting of ages ending in 0, 2, 5 and 8. For this reason, the single year of age
data for the male population as reported by the censuses, could not be used in calculat-
ing the working force participation rates by single years of age, which were needed for
estimating new entries and retirements.

        Furthermore the working force data which provide the numerators for the parti-
cipation rates were available only by five-year groups. Therefore in order to have working force participation by single years of age, the numbers of workers in each single
year of age had to be estimated by employing multipliers to subdivide for five-year age
groups. The single year of age labor force data provided by the multipliers were automatically smoothed; therefore they were not comparable with the irregular data for the
general male population by single years of age as provided by the censuses.

        Hence before working force participation rates could be computed, comparability
had to be achieved by smoothing the single year of age data for the population through
the application of multipliers to the five-year age group data for the male population.

Reasons For Using Census Survival Rates

As outlined previously, one of the components to be measured was the number of deaths occurring in each occupation for each five-year age cohort. For this purpose, decade survival rates were necessary. Under ideal conditions it would have been preferable to use intercensal working force life tables from which decade survival rates could have been computed. Aside from the fact that such tables were not available and their construction was beyond the scope of this project, other considerations also led to the decision that their use was not feasible. First of all, age cohorts were not exactly comparable from census to census because of age misreporting and the relative underenumeration of some age groups. The estimated number of survivors obtained by application of life table survival rates would in the case of many age cohorts have been widely at variance with the numbers actually observed at the following census and large-scale adjustments would have had to be made arbitrarily.

Net immigration, especially in the 1940s, was a further complicating factor which would have thrown off our estimation of deaths if decade survival rates had been calculated from life table data. Between 1940 and 1950 net immigration was 879,000, of which it is estimated that approximately 300,000 were males age 16 and over. While net immigration of males of working force age was only about 0.5 percent of all males of working force age, it is probable that the immigrants were concentrated in the younger ages rather than evenly distributed as to age. Also little reliable information was available on the occupational distribution of the immigrant working force.

If working force data had been tabulated according to nativity, the effect of immigration could have been eliminated by confining our study to the native population. Since this was not possible, the migration factor would in the case of some occupations and age cohorts have increased the discrepancy between expected and observed survivors if life table survival rates had been used to estimate survivors.

The decision was made therefore to estimate intercensal deaths by means of census survival rates, i.e., the numbers in the five-year age cohort at the end of the decade divided by the numbers in the five-year age cohort ten years younger at the beginning of the decade. The product of the census survival rate and the numbers in the working force for the corresponding age group at the beginning of the decade yields the estimated number of working force survivors at the end of the decade.

The assumption implicit in the application of census survival rates to working force data is that those in and outside of the working force undergo the same survival experiences. This is known not to be precisely the case. Nevertheless since at most ages the great majority of men are in the working force, the survival rate for all men in any specified cohort must be very similar to the survival rate for the men in the working force in that cohort.

It should be realized of course that deaths estimated by this procedure are net deaths, i.e., gross deaths plus or minus gains or losses due to migration, underenumeration and misreporting of age.

Survival Differentials by Occupation

The application of the same survival rates to all occupations within a specified cohort carries with it the further assumption that occupational survival differentials are negligible. The question of using occupational differentials was investigated, and it was found that the available literature was too fragmentary to be of any value. Accordingly it was finally decided that - considering available resources of time and labor - the most that could be done was to weight the census survival rates for the decade 1930 to 1940 by rural-urban differentials which would be applied respectively to agricultural occupations (farmers and farm managers, and farm laborers and foremen) and to nonagricultural occupations (the remaining eight major occupation categories). How these rural-urban differentials, which were based on 1939 rural and urban abridged life tables for the United States,[1] were calculated will be explained in detail presently.

Similar differentials were not employed for the decade 1940 to 1950 both because urban and rural life tables for that decade could not readily be had and also because the narrowing of urban and rural mortality differentials made it seem that this differential would be much less important in the 1940s than it had been in the 1930s.

In summary therefore for the decade 1930 to 1940 separate urban and rural census survival rates were used; for the 1940s the same census survival rates were used for all occupations.

Detailed Explanation of Census Survival Rate Construction

The general computational procedures. We turn now to a step-by-step explanation of the procedures involved in the construction of the census survival rates:

The first very simple step was the computation of total male census survival rates (without urban-rural differentials) for 1930-40 and 1940-50. These rates are shown in Table 14. For illustration purposes the cohort age 40 to 44 at the beginning of the decade will be used. For this cohort the computations were as follows:

$$\frac{\text{Males } 50 \text{ to } 54 \text{ in } 1940}{\text{Males } 40 \text{ to } 44 \text{ in } 1930} = \frac{3,752,750}{4,139,911} = .9065$$

$$\frac{\text{Males } 50 \text{ to } 54 \text{ in } 1950}{\text{Males } 40 \text{ to } 44 \text{ in } 1940} = \frac{4,128,658}{4,419,135} = .9343$$

It will be noted that .9065 and .9343 are the census survival rates on row (8) of Table 14. Since no urban-rural differentials were used for the 1940s, the calculations for this decade are now completed. The rest of this chapter is devoted to the process whereby the total census survival rate for 1930-40 was split into the separate urban and rural census survival rates (also shown in Table 14).

Computing urban and rural survival rates for the 1930s. In general what was done was to convert the four 1939 abridged life tables (viz., white and non-white males, urban and rural) into separate ten-year life table survival rates for five-year age cohorts. Then the white and non-white urban survival rates were combined to give total urban rates for each five-year age cohort. The white and non-white rural rates were similarly combined. The ratio of the rural to the urban survival rates yield a rural-urban differential which was applied to the ten-year census survival rates, due consideration being given to the proportion of males in each cohort living in rural and in urban areas. Of course it would have been preferable to use 1930-40 rural-urban life tables - or at least, 1935 life tables - but such tables were unavailable. The 1939 life tables were used as a reasonable approximation. Let us now follow through the actual details for the cohort age 40 to 44 in 1930.

1. The first three rows of Table 15 show the number of white male survivors to ages 40, 45, 50 and 55 out of 10,000 births for: (a) cities of 100,000 population and over, (b) other urban, and (c) rural. Dividing column (3) by column (1), and column (4) by column (2) for each region gives the probability at age 40 of surviving to age 50,

---

1. "U. S. Abridged Life Tables, 1939, Urban and Rural, By Regions, Color and Sex," FSA, Vol. 23, No. 15, June 30, 1947.

TABLE 14
CENSUS SURVIVAL RATES
(PROBABILITY OF FIVE-YEAR AGE COHORT SURVIVING FROM ONE CENSUS DATE TO THE NEXT)
BY URBAN AND RURAL FOR 1930 TO 1940

| Age at beginning of decade | Probability of surviving throughout decade | | | |
| | 1930-1940 | | | 1940-1950 |
	Total	Urban	Rural	
(1) 5 to 9 years	.9677	.9671	.9683	.9802
(2) 10 to 14 years	.9372	.9372	.9373	.9419
(3) 15 to 19 years	.9459	.9463	.9454	.9663
(4) 20 to 24 years	.9493	.9494	.9490	.9881
(5) 25 to 29 years	.9756	.9739	.9780	1.0123
(6) 30 to 34 years	.9679	.9637	.9741	1.0000
(7) 35 to 39 years	.8987	.8911	.9105	.9538
(8) 40 to 44 years	.9065	.8935	.9270	.9343
(9) 45 to 49 years	.8194	.8016	.8471	.8624
(10) 50 to 54 years	.7650	.7406	.8012	.8095
(11) 55 to 59 years	.7809	.7440	.8308	.8051
(12) 60 to 64 years	.6541	.6123	.7065	.6793

TABLE 15
COMPUTATION OF RURAL-URBAN LIFE TABLE SURVIVAL DIFFERENTIAL, 1930 TO 1940

White Males

| | | Age X | | | |
		40 (1)	45 (2)	50 (3)	55 (4)
(1) Number of	Cities 100,000+	.8763	.8457	.7995	.7344
(2) survivors	Other Urban	.8548	.8272	.7874	.7312
(3) out of 10,000	Rural	.8651	.8430	.8126	.7699
(4) Probability at age X	Cities 100,000+	.9124	.8684		
(5) of surviving 10 years	Other Urban	.9212	.8839		
(6) column (i) ÷ column (i-2)	Rural	.9393	.9133		
(7) Number of survivors out of 10,000	Urban	.8656	.8365	.7935	.7328
$\frac{\text{row (1) + row (2)}}{2}$					
(8) Probability at age X of surviving to Age X + 10 $\frac{\text{row (4) + row (5)}}{2}$	Urban	.9168	.8762		
(9) Probability at age X to X + 5	Urban	.8968			
(10) of surviving 10 years	Rural	.9265			
(11) Rural-urban survival differential row (10) ÷ row (9)		1.0331			

Non-White Males

(12) Probability at age X to X + 4 of surviving	Urban	.7758			
(13) 10 years	Rural	.8507			
(14) Rural-urban survival differential		1.0965			

and at age 45 of surviving to age 55. These probabilities are shown in rows (4), (5) and (6). For example, .8126 divided by .8651, the number of white male rural residents surviving to age 50, divided by the number of rural residents surviving to age 40, is equal to .9393, the probability at age 40 of a rural resident surviving to age 50.

2. In row (7) we have used a simple arithmetic average to combine for use in step 4 below the cities 100,000 and over and the other urban life table survivors. It was not thought necessary to use a weighted average because at the time of the 1940 census the total U. S. urban population was distributed approximately half and half among cities 100,000 and over and other urban.

3. In row (8) of Table 15 the probability of surviving ten years for total urban white males at ages 40 and 45 was computed by the unweighted average of the corresponding probabilities for cities 100,000 and over and other urban in rows (4) and (5). For example, one half of the sum of .9124 and .9219 is .9168 as shown in column (1) of row (8).

4. Rows (6) and (8) are respectively the white male rural and urban probabilities at ages 40 and 45 of surviving an additional ten years. In row (9) we have averaged (using as weights the number of urban survivors to age 40 and age 45 in row (7)) the urban probabilities at ages 40 and 45 of surviving ten years as shown in row (8) and called this average the probability of the white male urban cohort age 40 to 44 surviving ten years. This is equivalent to saying that the probability of a cohort age 40 to 44 surviving ten years approximately equals the probability at age 42½ of surviving ten years.

In row (10) the same procedure was applied to rows (6) and (3) to get the ten-year rural survival rate of a rural cohort age 40 to 44.

5. Row (11) - not actually made use of in subsequent computations - is the rural-urban ten-year survival differential derived by dividing row (10) by row (9).

6. Rows (12) to (14) in Table 15 show the life table survival rates and rural-urban differential obtained for non-white males when steps 1 through 5 were applied to the non-white male urban and rural life tables.

7. For subsequent use as weights the ratio of white to non-white males age 40 to 44 in urban and rural areas in 1940 was calculated. These ratios are shown in rows (1) and (2) of Table 16.

8. In row (3) of Table 16 we have combined (by means of a weighted average, with 9.7 and 1 as weights) the urban white and non-white ten-year life table survival rates into a total urban ten-year life table survival rate. In row (4) we obtained a total rural ten-year life table survival rate in the same manner, i.e., a weighted average of rows (10) and (13) from Table 15, with 8.90 and 1 as weights.

9. Row (5) of Table 16 shows the rural-urban ten-year life table survival differential obtained by dividing the rural ten-year survival rate in row (4) by the urban survival rate in row (3).

10. Row (6) is the ratio of rural males age 40 to 44 in the general population in 1940 to the urban males age 40 to 44.

11. We now have all the necessary ingredients for splitting the ten-year census survival rate in row (7) (from row (8) of Table 14) into separate urban and rural ten-year census survival rates. To take this final step, we note first the following two requirements:

a. We want the ratio of the rural to the urban ten-year census survival rates to be equal to 1.0375, the rural-urban ten-year life table survival differential for a cohort age 40 to 44 in 1930.

b. We want the total ten-year census survival rate to be equal to the average of the rural and urban ten-year census survival rates, each weighted according to its relative size in the total male population age 40 to 44, i.e., .629 and 1.0.

These two requirements can be expressed by the following two equations, using the row numbers of Table 16 as symbols:

$$\frac{(9)}{(8)} = (5)$$

$$\frac{(6)(9) + 1.0(8)}{(6) + 1.0} = (7)$$

where: (8) is the unknown urban census survival rate, (9) is the unknown rural census survival rate, and all the other terms are as listed in Table 16. Solving the set of equations for (8), the <u>urban</u> census survival rate, we get

$$(8) = \frac{(7)\left[(6) + 1.0\right]}{(5)(6) + 1.0}$$

The <u>rural</u> census survival rate follows immediately from $\frac{(9)}{(8)} = 5$ as soon as (8), the urban census survival rate, has been found. The urban and rural census survival rates in rows (8) and (9), it will be noted, are the same as those shown in Table 14, row (8), whose derivation it was the purpose of this section to explain.

TABLE 16
COMPUTATION OF URBAN AND RURAL CENSUS SURVIVAL RATES, 1930 TO 1940

		Age cohort 40-44
(1) Ratio of white to non-white males	Urban	9.78
(2) in 1940	Rural	8.90
(3) Life table probability of cohort	Urban	.8856
(4) surviving 10 years	Rural	.9188
(5) Rural-urban life table survival differential row (4) ÷ row (3)		1.0375
(6) Rural population age 40-44 ÷ urban population age 40-44		.629
(7) Census survival rate (urban and rural)		.9065
(8) Census survival	Urban	.8935
(9) rates	Rural	.9270

It will be recalled that our general model uses the balancing equation:

$$O_2 = O_1 - D + NE - R \pm NM$$

where O_2 and O_1 are the numbers observed in a given occupation and age cohort at the end and beginning of a decade, D is intercensal deaths among the occupational cohort, NE is intercensal new entries, R retirements, and NM net mobility. According to this equation the difference between the numbers observed in an occupational cohort at the end and at the beginning of a decade (occupational change) is attributable to one or more of the components of occupational change: deaths, new entries, retirements and net mobility. We want to estimate the magnitude of these components for each occupation and age cohort during the decade 1930 to 1940 and 1940 to 1950 in order to estimate their probable magnitude in the decade 1950 to 1960 and eventually to arrive at estimates of the 1960 occupational structure of the experienced civilian male working force.

In the last chapter our method for estimating intercensal deaths was described. In this chapter we take up intercensal new entry estimates by occupation and age cohort.

Stated in the most general way, our estimated new entries for a single year age cohort in a specified year is the difference between the occupational distribution of the cohort in the specified year and its estimated occupational distribution at the same time one year earlier, due allowance being made for mortality of course. The crux of the problem and of our method is the mode of estimating the occupational distribution of the cohort one year earlier. Let us explain our procedure with an illustration of 1939 new entry estimates, i.e., new entries between April 1, 1939, and April 1, 1940.

New Entries as of the Census Year

Procedures. Table 17 shows how new entries were estimated for the cohort age 18 in 1939, i.e., between April, 1939, and April, 1940, when the average age of the cohort changed from $17\frac{1}{2}$ to $18\frac{1}{2}$. Using multipliers, the occupation-age structure of the 1940 male working force and total male population had first been subdivided into single year of age data. With this information columns (2) and (4), the observed numbers by occupation for the cohorts age 17 and 18, could be immediately filled in. In column (3) the occupational working force participation rate, the proportion of all males age 17 in each occupation and in all occupations was then computed.

Now let us assume that those who were age 18 in 1940 and who had entered the working force at age 17 or younger had entered with the same occupational working force participation rates as those age 17 in 1940. We can then multiply these rates by the number of total males age 18 in 1940 (hence allowing for mortality between the ages 17 and 18) and obtain the expected numbers of the 18-year-old cohort in each and all occupations if there had been no new entries into the working force from this cohort during the past year. These expected numbers are shown in column (5).

The estimated number of new entries in column (6) was obtained by subtracting the expected (if there had been no new entries since the cohort reached age 17) from the observed at age 18.

Underlying assumptions. Let us consider the assumptions underlying the above procedures. In the first place the estimate of new entries is a net estimate in the sense that it makes no allowance for withdrawals (either temporary withdrawals or retirements); it represents gross new entries minus gross withdrawals. Secondly the validity of the new entry estimates rests in part upon the assumption that those age 18 in 1940 who entered the working force at age 17 or at earlier age had entered in substantially the same manner with respect to occupation as the cohort age 17 in 1940. While this assumption, barring sudden, drastic changes in the economy, is probably quite tenable, it

TABLE 17

COMPUTATION OF NEW ENTRIES INTO MALE WORKING FORCE BY OCCUPATION, 1939

COHORT AGE 18 IN 1939

(Numbers in thousands)

| Occupation | Age 17 | | Age 18 | | |
| | Observed | Participation rate1 | Observed | Expected2 | New entries3 |
(1)	(2)	(3)	(4)	(5)	(6)
(1) Professional, technical and kindred workers	1.2	.0010	5.6	1.2	+ 4.4
(2) Farmers and farm managers	4.8	.0038	16.2	4.7	+ 11.5
(3) Managers, officials and proprietors, except farm	1.4	.0011	3.1	1.4	+ 1.7
(4) Clerical and kindred workers	20.5	.0164	42.1	20.2	+ 21.9
(5) Sales workers	28.3	.0226	43.4	27.9	+ 15.5
(6) Craftsmen, foremen and kindred workers	60.5	.0484	122.1	59.7	+ 62.4
(7) Operatives and kindred workers	8.3	.0066	31.7	8.2	+ 23.5
(8) Service workers	32.9	.0263	42.0	32.5	+ 9.5
(9) Farm laborers and foremen	184.6	.1476	213.4	182.4	+ 31.0
(10) Laborers except farm and mine	64.3	.0514	135.4	63.5	+ 71.9
(11) All occupations	406.8	.3253	655.0	401.7	+253.3
(12) Total population	1250.5	1.0000	1234.8		

1. The observed number in each occupation divided by total male population age 17 in row (12) of column (2).
2. The total male population age 18 multiplied by each occupational participation rate at age 17 in column (3).
3. Column (4) - column (5).

TABLE 18

MAKING ADJUSTMENTS FOR NEW ENTRIES INTO MALE WORKING FORCE BY OCCUPATION, 1939

COHORT AGE 23 IN 1939

(Numbers in thousands)

Occupation (1)	New entries (unadjusted) (2)	New entries (adjusted)1 (3)
Professional, technical and kindred workers	+ 8.2	+ 6.6
Farmers and farm managers	+ 8.4	+ 6.8
Managers, officials and proprietors, except farm	+ 6.8	+ 5.5
Clerical and kindred workers	+ 2.4	+ 2.0
Sales workers	+ 3.2	+ 2.6
Craftsmen, foremen and kindred workers	+ 13.0	+ 10.5
Operatives and kindred workers	+ 10.0	+ 8.1
Service workers	+ 2.5	+ 2.0
Farm laborers and foremen	- 10.6	-
Laborers except farm and mine	+ 1.3	+ 1.4
All occupations	+ 45.2	+ 45.2

1. Multiplying each entry in column (2) by .810035, the result of $\frac{45.2}{45.2 + 10.6}$, where 45.2 + 10.6 equals sum of plus entries in column (2).

nonetheless remains an assumption. It is not important, however, to dwell upon the point because in estimating <u>intercensal</u> new entries a modification was introduced the implications of which will be taken up at the appropriate place.

Finally we have assumed that the difference between observed and expected can only take place through gross new entries and gross withdrawals (deaths already having been allowed for); the assumption has been made implicitly that the effect of the fourth component, net mobility, was nil or negligible during the year interval. This assumption is absolutely sound when all occupations (the total working force participation of the cohort) are considered, for in this case the plus and minus net mobilities among the different occupations cancel one another out. Hence our estimate of total new entries into the working force from the age cohort is unaffected by net mobility.

But when we come to the distribution of these total new entries among the various occupations, we are on less solid ground. Evidently our estimate of new entries is a net estimate in the further respect that it signifies the gain through gross new entries plus or minus the gain or loss through net mobility - as well as minus the loss through gross withdrawals.

Suppose, however, the gain by new entries is offset by an even greater loss via net mobility (and gross retirements). This situation actually occurred in some instances. Table 18 showing new entries in 1939 for the cohort age 23 illustrates the point. Farm laborers and foremen, presumably including much unpaid family labor, showed a loss of 10.6 thousands through new entries. It is obvious that the important factor here was not gross retirements but the net mobility of the young leaving the farm and moving to other occupations.

Some adjustment was called for. Since the total new entries of 45.2 thousands was unaffected by net mobility, this figure should remain the same. However, the estimate of new entries for each of the occupations except farm laborers had been swollen because of net mobility from farm labor. It seemed reasonable to say that new entries into farm laborers was zero (instead of negative) and then, in order not to change the total of 45.2 thousand new entries, to reduce the plus new entries of the other occupations by 10.6 thousand all told. No other basis being available for allocating the reduction among the occupations, the simplest procedure seemed to be to prorate the reduction for each occupation according to its unadjusted volume of new entries. The formula presented in footnote 1 of Table 18 accomplishes this operation with a minimum amount of computation.

A final statement of what is meant by new entries as herein used can now be made: an estimate of new entries signifies gross new entries minus gross retirements, plus or minus net mobility, minus the distributed difference between net mobility and new entries of those occupations which gain less through new entries than they lose through net mobility.

While the total volume of new entries represents net new entries in the usual sense of the word (gross new entries minus gross retirements), new entries for individual occupations is seen to be a much more complicated concept, one whose meaning is not easily grasped intuitively - at least, for those ages where net mobility is a factor of any great consequence. It is worth stating again, however, that the unusual meaning of the concept does not affect its usefulness for making projections. This is so because it is the net resultant of these various factors that we want to project, not the individual ones.

<u>Age limits for new entries.</u> So as to determine at what age new entries dwindled off and became sufficiently small that they could be disregarded for projection purposes, estimates of new entries were computed from age 14 through age 29 for each of the three census years, 1930, 1940 and 1950. It was found that they became negligible

after age 24. Accordingly it was decided that new entries would be introduced only
through age 24 both in the study of past occupational change and also in making projections.

New Entries During a Decade

     General procedures. The application of our operational definition of new en-
tries required occupational working force participation rates for each single year as
well as intercensal estimates of the male population by single years of age. The intercensal population estimates were obtained from the Census Bureau, and the intercensal
participation rates were estimated by linear interpolation of the census year participation rates.

     As an example of the procedures let us consider the estimation of new entries
during the 1940s for the cohort age 7 in 1940. This cohort began to enter the working
force at age 14 in 1947 and contributed additional new entries at age 15 in 1947 (April,
1947, to April, 1948), at age 16 in 1948, and at age 17 in 1949. What had to be done in
effect was first to estimate the new entries at age 14 in the year April, 1946, to March,
1947, inclusive by applying the estimated occupational participation rates for age 14 to
the estimated population age 14 in 1947. These would all be new entries so that expected
and observed would be identical at age 14.

     For those age 15 in April, 1948, the expected would be the estimated participa-
tion rates for age 14 in 1947 times the estimated population age 15 in 1948, the observed
would be the estimated rates for age 15 in 1948 times the estimated population age 15 in
1948; the difference between observed and expected would be the estimated new entries at
age 15 in 1947. In similar manner new entry estimates for age 16 in 1948 and age 17 in
1949 would be obtained.

     Note that the operational definition of new entries used for census year new
entries has now been slightly modified for estimating intercensal new entries. For census year new entries the assumption was made that those in age group 18 in 1940 who had
entered the working force before they were 18 had had the same participation rates the
year before, 1939, as the cohort age 17 in 1940 had in 1940. Such an assumption is no
longer necessary when we have estimates of participation rates for each single year of
age for each intercensal year. In fact of course we have merely replaced one assumption
with another, the assumed empirical validity of our estimated intercensal occupational
participation rates.

     In any event having obtained estimates of new entries at age 14 in 1946, age
15 in 1947, etc., those new entries would then have to be survived to 1950 from their
year of entry into the working force. We are concerned only with those intercensal new
entries who survive to the end of the decade. Those who do not survive have no place in
the balancing equation since they have no effect on O_2, the observed number in an occupation at the end of the decade.

     Applied procedures. Estimating intercensal new entries in this way would have
been exceedingly laborious and in fact was not necessary. An equivalent and computation-
ally much simpler procedure was devised as illustrated in Table 19 with the cohort age 7
in 1940. Instead of the intercensal population estimates, the size of the cohort in 1940
was used throughout. Consequently estimates were obtained of new entries under the assumption that no deaths occurred to the cohort during the decade. The sum of all these
estimates could then be survived all at once with the ten-year census survival rates.

     In column (2) to (5) the observed, ages 14 to 17 in 1947 to 1950, were obtained
from the product of the total population age 7 in 1940 and the participation rates of
ages 14, 15, 16 and 17 in 1947, 1948, 1949 and 1950. These observed, be it remembered,
are the numbers which would have been observed had there been no deaths to the cohort

TABLE 19
COMPUTATION OF UNSURVIVED
NEW ENTRIES INTO MALE
WORKING FORCE BY
OCCUPATION, 1940-50
COHORT AGE 7 IN 1940
(Numbers in thousands)

Occupation	Observed Age 14 1947 (Expected) (Age 15) (1948)	Observed Age 15 1948 (Expected) (Age 16) (1949)	Observed Age 16 1949 (Expected) (Age 17) (1950)	Observ Age 1950
(1)	(2)	(3)	(4)	(5)
Professional, technical and kindred workers	3.1	3.2	2.5	3.9
Farmers and farm managers	2.3	3.1	6.5	11.9
Managers, officials and proprietors, except farm	1.0	1.4	1.8	2.
Clerical and kindred workers	.8	4.0	8.2	27.
Sales workers	29.0	32.5	34.7	40.
Craftsmen, foremen and kindred workers	5.2	14.2	33.1	83.
Operatives and kindred workers	1.4	2.8	5.3	20.
Service workers	6.1	16.3	32.9	38.
Farm laborers and foremen	51.2	85.7	121.2	132.
Laborers except farm and mine	6.7	16.0	35.8	64.
All occupations	106.8	179.2	282.0	424.

Total male population in 1940
1058.9

New entries

Age 14 1946 (1) (6)	Age 15 1947 (2)-(1) (7)	Age 16 1948 (3)-(2) (8)	Age 16 1948 Adjusted (9)	Age 17 1949 (4)-(3) (10)	Age 14-17 1946-49 (5)+(6)+ (8)+(9) (11)
3.1	.1	-.7	–	1.4	4.6
2.3	.8	3.4	3.4	5.4	11.9
1.0	.4	.4	.4	.5	2.3
.8	3.2	4.2	4.2	19.0	27.2
29.0	3.5	2.2	2.2	5.6	40.3
5.2	9.0	18.9	18.8	50.8	83.8
1.4	1.4	2.5	2.5	15.4	20.7
6.1	10.2	16.6	16.5	5.6	38.4
51.2	34.5	35.5	35.2	10.8	131.7
6.7	9.3	19.8	19.6	28.3	63.9
106.8	72.4	102.8	102.8	142.8	424.8

since the 1940 census. These observed, however, are also the expected one year older and one year later. That is, the observed age 15 in 1948 is the same as could be expected one year later had there been no further new entries during that last year. Hence estimates of new entries at each subsequent year can be had simply by subtracting from each column the entries in the column preceding it. Column (2) of course is an exception since the observed at age 14 presumably are all new entries at age 14. Also since a negative new entry figure appears for age 16 in 1948, professional workers in column (8) had to be adjusted as shown in column (9) and as explained in Table 18.

Similar computations were made for all single year cohorts from age 5 to age 23 in 1940, cohort age 24 in 1940 having already entered at age 24 prior to the 1940 census. Then the new entries by single year cohorts were grouped together in five-year cohorts. How census survival rates were applied to these unsurvived new entry estimates will be explained in Chapter 13.

Considerations underlying these procedures. Before closing this chapter, we should consider further the empirical validity of estimating intercensal occupational working force participation by linear interpolation. The first observation to be made is that, regardless of how the intercensal rates are estimated, the total volume of intercensal new entries remains unaffected. For a cohort less than age 14 in 1940, total new entries in the decade 1940 to 1950 always equals the observed in 1950; and for a cohort 14 or over in 1940, total new entries always equals the first observed column subtracted from the last observed column.

Furthermore this observation will be true for each occupation (not just for all occupations together) wherever the cohort experiences no negative new entries during the intercensal period. The presence of negative new entries forces a readjustment downward in all the positive new entries. Only to the extent that negative entries crop up does it make a difference how intercensal participation rates are estimated. At the same time attention should be called to the fact that negative new entries can sometimes be of fairly large magnitude.

The problem is best approached by considering a concrete extreme case in which linear interpolation was most likely to be an unrealistic description of what actually happened – the period 1940 to 1945 when the Second World War dislocated the whole occupational structure. During this period it is known that large numbers of young men withdrew from the civilian working force to join the armed forces and re-entered the civilian working force after the war. While this movement is not detected by linear interpolation of censal participation rates, it is fortunately not relevant to our analysis. We are interested in change in working force and occupational status between the two census dates. Our model was not intended to catch post-censal change which was followed by a reversion to original status by the time of the next census. And those who later returned to the working force but in a different occupation will be detected in our analysis of net mobility.

A more complicated problem is presented by those young men who entered the working force for the first time after the 1940 census with some wartime occupation such as operative or craftsman, then withdrew to join the armed forces and finally re-entered the civilian working force prior to the 1950 census with some other occupation such as clerical worker, professional worker or farm laborer. This is movement that our model wants to detect – new entries during the intercensal period who at the end of the decade had a different occupation from that at the time they entered. Yet net mobility from occupation of entry cannot be correctly estimated unless occupation of entry also be estimated correctly. And occupation of entry will probably not be correctly estimated for the years 1941 to 1945 if working force participation rates are assumed to be an orderly linear development between the 1940 and 1950 rates.

Ways and means out of the dilemma were investigated. The Census Current Population Survey sample estimates of working force participation rates for the entire decade were closely examined and found insufficient for our purposes. These data were not available tabulated both by age and by occupation simultaneously. It was clear that the estimation of intercensal occupational working force participation rates via the Current Population Survey data or by any method other than linear interpolation would have been just as arbitrary and even less satisfactory because unsystematic.

An equally decisive consideration for the retention of linearly interpolated rates was that the set of 1960 projections based on the experience of the 1940s was intended to indicate what the occupational structure of the male working force would be in 1960 if the decade 1950 to 1960 were a period without war. From this point of view, the war years of the 1940s were abnormal. Hence allowance for this abnormality would have to be made in projecting to 1960 if our description of the patterns of occupational change in the 1940s included the extraordinary changes that occurred during the war and the subsequent readjustment after the war. The use of linearly interpolated estimates of rates, in effect, means that allowance has been made for the wartime abnormality by not taking it into consideration in the first place.

One further implication of the linearly interpolated intercensal participation rates should be observed. Since 1940 was a time of large-scale unemployment and relatively depressed economic conditions, and 1950 was a period of prosperity, linearly interpolated rates serve to describe the decade as one of gradual transition from bad times to good times – in short as a period of great change. On the other hand, the decade 1950 to 1960 is scarcely likely to witness changes of such magnitude if 1960 is a prosperous year because 1950 was also prosperous. The decade of the 1950s would not be a decade of transition like the 1940s. The set of 1960 projections which assumes the 1950s will parallel the economic conditions of the 1940s would be most usefully interpreted as the upper limit on the amount and kinds of change likely to take place.

Since retirements are new entries in reverse, our model for estimating retirements - either as of a census year or intercensal - is the same as our new entries estimation model with, however, a slight variation. Once this variation is understood, almost everything that was said in the last chapter about new entries applies to retirements and therefore need not be repeated.

Retirements as of the Census Year

Table 20, showing retirements at age 64 in the year prior to the 1940 census, is analogous with Tables 17 and 18 and should be compared with them. Computations were exactly the same with one exception: in the case of retirements, the observed are subtracted from the expected whereas new entries were estimated by subtracting the expected from the observed.

The logic of the method is to assume that those age 64 in 1940 had the same occupational participation rates when age 63 in 1939 as did those age 63 in 1940; then multiplying these rates by the number of males age 64 in 1940 gives the expected distribution at age 64 in 1940 if no retirements had taken place in the intervening year (and if net mobility had been negligible); finally, the excess of expected over observed represents the change accounted for by retirements.

Like new entries, the number of retirements is a net figure. Total retirements (retirements from the working force as a whole) are actually gross retirements minus whatever gross new entries or re-entries may have occurred. Retirements for particular occupations are also affected by gains or losses through net mobility; the distribution of total retirements among the various occupations can be described as net retirements in the conventional sense only if net mobility is very small. Fortunately the volume of net mobility is much smaller at the older ages so that net retirements by occupation as here used probably represent - much better than do net new entries - what the layman understands by the term.

On the other hand, the phenomenon of negative retirements - analogous to negative new entries - is found because for some occupations (especially farm laborers and foremen and service workers) the volume of retirements is so small that more workers are gained through net mobility than are lost through retirements. An instance of this is shown for farm laborers in column (6) of Table 20; the adjusted retirement figures of column (7) were arrived at in exactly the same way as new entry estimates were adjusted in Table 18.

Starting with age 74 and working backwards, retirements were estimated for each of three census years, 1930, 1940 and 1950. It was found that the volume of retirements prior to age 51 was sufficiently small so as not to have to be taken into account as a significant component of occupational change.

Retirements During a Decade

Intercensal occupational working force participation rates were estimated for each single year of age from 51 through 74 and for each intercensal year for both the 1930s and 1940s. Estimation of the rates was by linear interpolation in precisely the same way as was done for new entries.

Beginning with the cohort age 41 in 1930 (or in 1940 when estimating retirements during the 1940s) and continuing through the cohort age 64 in 1930, the retirements of a cohort were estimated for each year between 1931 and 1940 inclusive (or 1941 to 1940 inclusive for the 1940s) in which the cohort was not younger than 51 or older than 74. Thus the cohort age 41 in 1930 began retiring at age 51 in the year 1939, i.e., April, 1939, to April, 1940. And the cohort age 64 in 1930 was still retiring at age 74 in 1939

TABLE 20

COMPUTATION OF RETIREMENTS FROM MALE WORKING FORCE BY OCCUPATION, 1939

COHORT AGE 64 IN 1939

(Numbers in thousands)

| Occupation | Age 63 | | Age 64 | | Retire- ments (5)-(4) | Retire- ments Adjusted |
| | Observed | Partici- pation rate | Observed | Expected | | |
(1)	(2)	(3)	(4)	(5)	(6)	(7)
Professional, technical and kindred workers	18.5	.0405	16.8	17.8	+ 1.0	+ 1.0
Farmers and farm managers	84.7	.1852	80.0	81.3	+ 1.3	+ 1.3
Managers, officials and proprietors, except farm	41.6	.0910	37.2	39.9	+ 2.7	+ 2.6
Clerical and kindred workers	15.3	.0335	13.0	14.7	+ 1.7	+ 1.7
Sales workers	16.3	.0356	14.5	15.6	+ 1.1	+ 1.1
Craftsmen, foremen and kindred workers	57.7	.1262	50.9	55.4	+ 4.5	+ 4.4
Operatives and kindred workers	35.8	.0783	31.1	34.4	+ 3.3	+ 3.2
Service workers	27.1	.0593	24.6	26.0	+ 1.4	+ 1.4
Farm laborers and foremen	16.3	.0356	15.9	15.6	- .3	-
Laborers except farm and mine	36.6	.0800	33.6	35.1	+ 1.5	+ 1.5
All occupations	349.9	.7652	317.6	335.8	+ 18.2	+ 18.2
Total population	457.3	-	438.9	-	-	-

Because working force participation rates by single year of age beyond age 74 could not easily be obtained from available data for cohorts older than 64 in 1930, it was necessary to assume that all had either died or retired by the end of the decade.

The process of estimating intercensal retirements was the same as for estimating intercensal new entries (see Table 19) except, as already explained, the observed were subtracted from the expected instead of the expected being subtracted from the observed.

As in the case of new entries, the question arose of the empirical validity of using linearly interpolated occupational working force participation rates for the disturbed years of the Second World War for estimating intercensal retirements. An analysis of Current Population Survey reports showed that total working force participation rates rose during the war years for those age 45 to 64. No further subdivision by age was available, but it was felt that part of this increase could be attributed to deferred retirements especially among the younger men in this broad age category. Somewhat arbitrarily therefore it was decided to exclude retirements at ages 51 to 54 in the years 1941 to 1946.

Having reached the fourth and last of our components of occupational change, net mobility, let us recapitulate where we stand. It will be recalled that net mobility was estimated residually from the balancing equation, (1) $O_2 = O_1 - D + NE - R \pm NM$. Re-arranging the balancing equation into the form: (2) $\pm NM = O_2 - O_1 + D - NE + R$, the net mobility in each occupation in each decade for each five-year age cohort can be estimated by filling in the terms on the right-hand side of the equation.

We cannot as yet, however, fill in the terms on the right-hand side. In the two preceding chapters we described how the numbers of new entries and retirements had been estimated on the assumption that there had been no deaths among the cohort during the decade in question.

Three steps yet remain before the balancing equation can be used to estimate net mobility: (1) O_1, the observed number at the beginning of the decade, must be survived to the end of the decade via application of the census survival rates so as to obtain the estimated number of deaths. (2) The unsurvived new entries and retirements must also be survived to the end of the decade inasmuch as the terms NE and R of the balancing equation obviously designate only those who entered (or retired) and survived to the end of the decade. Those who entered but died before the next census have no effect on occupational change as of the terminal points of the decade, and those who retired but died are counted as dead rather than retired at the time of second census. (3) An adjustment must be made in the estimated number of deaths to allow for differential survival experience between the total male population and those participating in the working force, our census survival rates being those of the general male population.

Tables 21, 22 and 23 illustrate the procedure adopted. Three different tables are required because the balancing equation can be simplified in three different ways when specific age cohorts are analyzed. No one five-year age cohort is being exposed simultaneously to all four components of occupational change. Cohorts never younger than 25 throughout a decade are not exposed to new entries, and cohorts never older than 51 are not exposed to retirements. Consequently the cohorts age 25 to 29, 30 to 34 and 35 to 39 at the beginning of a decade are being exposed neither to new entries nor to retirements. For these three cohorts, the terms NE and R drop out of the balancing equations; for all cohorts younger than these three the term R drops out; and finally, the term NE disappears for all older cohorts.

Computing Net Mobility For Cohorts Under Age 25

An example is given in Table 21 where the steps that were taken for the cohort age 15 to 19 in the decade 1931 to 1940 are shown. Steps 1 and 2 mentioned above, the surviving of O_1 and of the unsurvived new entries, were combined into one operation by adding them together in column (4) and then multiplying the sum by the census survival rates[1] to get in column (5) the expected number in 1950 under the assumption of no intercensal net mobility. Arithmetically this operation is exactly identical to that of multiplying O_1 and the unsurvived NE separately by the survival rates and then summing the results. The expected in 1940 therefore represents the survivors of the observed in 1930 plus the survived new entries. Since whatever retirements occurred at this age are subsumed under new entries (net new entries is equal to gross new entries minus gross retirements), any difference found between expected in 1940 and observed in 1940 can be attributed to net mobility.

---

1. The ten-year census survival rates used here are taken from row (3) of Table 14.

TABLE 21
COMPUTATION OF NET MOBILITY OF MALE
WORKING FORCE BY OCCUPATION, 1930-40
COHORT AGE 15 TO 19 IN 1930
(Numbers in thousands)

Occupation	Observed 1930 (O_1)
(1)	(2)
Professional, technical and kindred workers	28.4
Farmers and farm managers	48.5
Managers, officials and proprietors, except farm	23.8
Clerical and kindred workers	249.3
Sales workers	149.1
Craftsmen, foremen and kindred workers	144.4
Operatives and kindred workers	520.9
Service workers	103.1
Farm laborers and foremen	1031.2
Laborers except farm and mine	435.0
All occupations	2733.7

TABLE 22
COMPUTATION OF NET MOBILITY OF MALE
WORKING FORCE BY OCCUPATION, 1940-50
COHORT AGE 30 TO 34 IN 1940
(Numbers in thousands)

Occupation	Observed, 1940 (O_1)
(1)	(2)
Professional, technical and kindred workers	380.2
Farmers and farm managers	503.3
Managers, officials and proprietors, except farm	394.5
Clerical and kindred workers	318.5
Sales workers	303.7
Craftsmen, foremen and kindred workers	751.0
Operatives and kindred workers	1055.0
Service workers	262.1
Farm laborers and foremen	274.7
Laborers except farm and mine	574.0
All occupations	4817.0

Unsurvived new entries, 1930-39 (NE) (3)	$(O_1 \div NE)$ $(2) \div (3)$ (4)	Expected[1] 1940 (5)	Observed 1940 (O_2) (6)	Expected[2] 1940 (Adjusted) (7)	Net Mobility (6)-(7) (8)
174.1	202.5	191.6	355.2	192.2	+ 163.0
278.3	326.8	309.0	455.8	310.0	+ 145.8
134.5	158.3	149.8	283.2	150.3	+ 132.9
172.0	421.3	398.7	374.4	400.0	- 25.6
162.8	311.9	295.2	335.2	296.2	+ 39.0
407.2	551.6	522.0	636.8	523.8	+ 113.0
603.5	1124.4	1064.0	1238.0	1067.6	+ 170.4
130.9	234.0	221.4	272.3	222.1	+ 50.2
171.0	1202.2	1136.6	441.7	1140.5	- 698.8
406.4	841.4	796.2	709.0	798.9	- 89.9
2640.7	5374.4	5084.5	5101.6	5101.6	-

1. Multiplying column (4) by census survival rates - .9454 for Farmers and farm managers and Farm laborers and foremen, .9463 for all the other occupations.
2. Multiplying column (5) by 5101.6 ÷ 5084.5 = 1.0033

Expected, 1950 (3)	Observed, 1950 (O_2) (4)	Expected, 1950 (Adjusted) (5)	Net mobility (4)-(5) (6)
380.2	392.1	373.7	+ 18.4
503.3	485.6	494.6	- 9.0
394.5	637.9	387.7	+ 250.2
318.5	266.4	313.0	- 46.6
303.7	269.7	298.5	- 28.8
751.0	1000.0	738.1	+ 261.9
1055.0	941.0	1036.9	- 95.9
262.1	263.1	257.6	+ 5.5
274.7	124.4	270.0	- 145.6
574.0	354.0	564.1	- 210.1
4817.0	4734.2	4734.2	-

1. Multiplying column (2) by census survival rate of 1.0000, i.e., row (6) of Table 14.
2. Multiplying column (3) by 4734.2 ÷ 4817.0 = .9828

TABLE 23

COMPUTATION OF NET MOBILITY OF MALE WORKING FORCE BY OCCUPATION, 1940-50

COHORT AGE 55 TO 59 IN 1940

(Numbers in thousands)

Occupation	Observed 1940 (O_1)	Unsurvived retirements, 1941-50 (R)	(O_1 - R) (2)-(3)	Expected[1] 1950	Observed 1950 (O_2)	Expected[2] 1950 (adjusted)	Net mobility (6)-(7)
(1)	(2)	(3)	(4)	(5)	(6)	(7)	(8)
Professional, technical and kindred workers	131.3	35.2	96.1	77.4	80.5	77.5	+ 3.0
Farmers and farm managers	530.5	166.2	364.3	293.3	285.0	293.9	- 8.9
Managers, officials and proprietors, except farm	318.8	101.9	216.9	174.6	172.5	174.9	- 2.4
Clerical and kindred workers	104.9	33.0	71.9	57.9	69.8	58.0	+ 11.8
Sales workers	132.5	30.0	102.5	82.5	81.1	82.7	- 1.6
Craftsmen, foremen and kindred workers	482.7	171.8	310.9	250.3	246.5	250.8	- 4.3
Operatives and kindred workers	330.8	116.3	214.5	172.7	169.9	173.0	- 3.1
Service workers	177.8	15.9	161.9	130.3	151.4	130.5	+ 20.9
Farm laborers and foremen	118.9	33.5	85.4	68.8	65.2	68.9	- 3.7
Laborers except farm and mine	312.8	146.3	166.5	134.1	122.7	134.4	- 11.7
All occupations	2641.0	850.1	1790.9	1441.9	1444.6	1444.6	

1. Multiplying column (4) by census survival rate of .8051, i.e., row (11) of Table 14.
2. Multiplying column (5) by 1444.6 ÷ 1441.9 = 1.0019

Or rather it could be attributed to net mobility if those in the working force in this age cohort had had the same survival experience as those not in the working force. Because they did not, a slight discrepancy obtained between the total expected and the total observed in the working force at the end of the decade. This difference was adjusted, as indicated in footnote 2 of Table 21, by prorating it among the several occupations according to their size.

Now the balancing equation can be brought in. (2) can be re-written as: (3) $\pm NM = O_2 - (O_1 - D + NE - R)$, where in the case of this particular cohort R does not appear. Noting that the parenthetical term of (3), $O_1 - D + NE$, is equal to survivors of O_1 plus surviving new entries which, in turn is equal to the expected in 1940 in column (7), we can write the balancing equation as:

$\pm NM = O_2 -$ Expected in 1940

$= $ column (6) $-$ column (7) $=$ column (8)

Computing Net Mobility For Cohorts Age 25 and Over

The estimations of net mobility for the cohort 30 to 34 in 1940 (Table 22) and for the cohort age 55 to 59 in 1940 (Table 23) are similar to those shown in Table 21. In Table 22 everything is exactly the same except that new entries are nil and the rural-urban census survival differentials are not used for the decade 1940 to 1950. And in Table 23 the unsurvived retirements have to be subtracted from O_1 (instead of being added like the unsurvived new entries) before application of the census survival rate.

Operational Definition of Net Mobility

A word or two needs to be said about the precise meaning of net mobility as estimated here. In the chapter on New Entries, it was pointed out that estimated new entries for an individual occupation means in actuality gross new entries minus gross retirements, plus or minus the gain or loss through net mobility (except in the case where for one or more occupations the loss via net mobility is greater than the gain via new entries). A careful examination of the matter[2] reveals that a cohort would have virtually no net mobility at all in a decade if it passed through each year of the decade without one of its occupations having lost more through net mobility than it gained through new entries, i.e., without ever having any negative new entries. For example, in Table 19 the cohort age 7 in 1940 would have as its estimated unsurvived new entries the same figures as in column (4), the unsurvived observed in 1950. Hence when single year cohorts were combined into five-year cohorts and census survival rates were applied, we would find that expected and observed in 1950 were virtually identical.[3] Net mobility would therefore be very small since it is estimated by the difference between expected and observed at the end of the decade.

Similarly if the cohorts undergoing retirements in every year of the decade, i.e., the cohorts age 50 to 54 and older at the beginning of the decade, had no negative retirements among any of their occupations throughout the decade, they would have no net mobility.

---

2. This analysis of the relation of net mobility to new entries applies only to cohorts 24 years of age or less at the end of the decade. Since older cohorts are not exposed to working force entrance during those intercensal years when they are older than 24, only part of its net mobility derives from negative new entries.

3. They would be exactly identical for the decade 1940 to 1950 to the extent that there were no occupational survival differentials.

Another way of looking at it may be illuminating. Net mobility was said to be estimated by the difference between expected and observed at the end of the decade. Actually, however, it was estimated as the second difference between expected and observed, since new entries (or retirements) were also estimated, and prior to net mobility, as the difference between expected and observed. Net mobility is very largely the difference that is left over after the first difference has been eliminated, and the difference that is left over after the first difference has been taken exists[4] only by virtue of the redistribution of negative new entries (or retirements) among the several occupations.

This analysis of net mobility is not applicable to the cohorts which were not exposed to new entries or retirements during the decade, the cohorts age 25 to 29, 30 to 34 and 35 to 39 at the beginning of the decade.[5] In the case of these cohorts net mobility has the more usual meaning of gross gain minus gross loss through net mobility - modified to some slight extent, however, by small gains and losses due to new entries and retirements not having been taken into account.

This definition of net mobility, although somewhat different from the popular definition of the term, nevertheless is entirely usable for the projection purposes - the ultimate aim of these models. It is the net resultant of all the changes which occur among a cohort of men during a decade that is the important consideration. Whether these changes are subsumed under the headings of new entries or retirements or net mobility is of less consideration. The changes were studied in terms of their individual components so as to be able to apply the components separately in the projections.

Therefore our inability to distinguish clearly among the components is of but secondary importance. Consider this example: a 55 year old operative in 1940 becomes a craftsman in 1942 and remains in this category through 1950. Meanwhile a 55 year old craftsman in 1940 retires from the working force in 1948. The two individuals cancel each other out; there has been neither addition to nor a subtraction from the craftsman category. Therefore in making our component analysis, we would say that there had been no change in the craftsman group for this age cohort between the terminal dates. This is the fact of prime consideration, for in making our projections a decade hence, to 1960, we are concerned primarily with the net data as of the terminal period and not as of any of the intervening years, and only incidentally with those movements which canceled each other out.

---

4. With the exception of that difference attributable to those occupational survival differentials for which our model has not been able to make provision.

5. Furthermore it is applicable only in part to those cohorts (age 15 to 24 and 40 to 49 at the beginning of decade) which were exposed to either new entries or retirements only during some of the intercensal years.

CHAPTER 14

OCCUPATIONAL CHANGE PATTERNS SUMMARIZED

In this chapter we take the final step in the estimation of the components of occupational change in the balancing equations and then use these balancing equations to summarize the patterns of occupational change in the past two decades: (a) by age cohort and by occupation within each age cohort and (b) by occupation and by age cohort within each occupation.

Our explanation of how intercensal deaths were estimated for each age cohort by occupation remains incomplete up to this point. In the last chapter census survival rates were applied to the sum of the observed at the beginning of the decade and unsurvived intercensal new entries (or to the difference between the observed and unsurvived intercensal retirements); then the resulting expected at the end of the decade had to be adjusted slightly on account of the difference between the survival experience of those in and those not in the labor force. We now need an estimate of intercensal deaths which refers only to the observed at the beginning of the decade (O_1) and which at the same time takes into account the adjustment made because of the survival differential. The obvious procedure was to raise or lower each O_1 by the adjustment factor (observed at end of decade divided by expected at end of decade) and then multiply by the appropriate census survival rate, thereby obtaining the survivors of O_1. The required estimate of deaths is of course those who did not survive. The estimate of survived new entries (the term NE of the balancing equation) was obtained in similar fashion.

Table 24 shows how this was done and, more importantly, summarizes in balancing equation form the components of occupational change for one of the cohorts in one of the two decades. For each row of Table 24 the balancing equation is: column (2) = column (3) - column (4) + column (8) ± column (9). With the data summarized in this way, it becomes possible either to compare the experiences of the same age group in the two decades or to take each age cohort and trace through its history of occupational change from 1930 to 1950.

Finally balancing equation summarizations were made for each major occupational category by five-year age cohorts for each decade. This permits analysis of different patterns of change by age within each occupation. Craftsmen and foremen by age during the 1930s are shown in Table 25.[1]

---

1. Because available data on males in the labor force 75 and over were insufficiently detailed for the estimation of retirements by our model, component analysis does not cover those over 74. For the sake of completeness, however, the cohorts age 75 to 79 and 80 to 84 at the end of the decade (since they were not over 74 at the beginning of the decade) are included in this summary table and are arbitrarily assumed all to be either dead or retired. Deaths were estimated by census survival rates and the rest were counted as retirements. Actually, however, some 18 percent of males 75 and over were in the working force in both 1940 and 1950. In both instances this represented an insignificant proportion of the total male working force.

TABLE 24
COMPONENTS OF OCCUPATIONAL CHANGE
IN MALE WORKING FORCE, 1940-50
COHORT AGE 15 TO 19 IN 1940
(Numbers in thousands)

Occupation	Observed 1950 (O_2)	Observed 1940 (O_1)	Deaths (D)
(1)	(2)	(3)	(4)
Professional, technical and kindred workers	499.0	19.7	.3
Farmers and farm managers	374.6	52.6	.8
Managers, officials and proprietors, except farm	346.6	11.3	.2
Clerical and kindred workers	413.5	127.4	2.1
Sales workers	380.5	151.4	2.5
Craftsmen, foremen and kindred workers	1002.9	94.6	1.6
Operatives and kindred workers	1295.4	374.1	6.1
Service workers	235.4	135.6	2.2
Farm laborers and foremen	216.0	834.7	13.6
Laborers except farm and mine	450.0	374.9	6.1
All occupations	5213.9	2176.3	35.5
Total population	5972.1	6180.1	–

TABLE 25
COMPONENTS OF OCCUPATIONAL CHANGE IN MALE WORKING FORCE, 1930-40
CRAFTSMEN, FOREMEN AND KINDRED WORKERS
(Numbers in thousands)

Age in 1930	Observed in 1940 (O_2)	Observed in 1930 (O_1)	Deaths (D)
(1)	(2)	(3)	(4)
0 - 4	.2	–	–
5 - 9	94.6	–	–
10 - 14	459.5	.1	–
15 - 19	636.8	144.4	7.3
20 - 24	751.0	633.6	32.8
25 - 29	806.9	791.4	29.5
30 - 34	781.3	820.6	51.3
35 - 39	749.0	870.3	129.1
40 - 44	659.5	782.6	113.6
45 - 49	482.7	670.4	141.0
50 - 54	320.7	529.7	133.3
55 - 59	164.5	384.1	91.4
60 - 64	56.9	272.9	107.7
65 - 69	–	158.2	77.5
70 - 74	–	70.0	44.7
Total	5963.6	6128.3	959.2

Survivors[1] to 1950	Unsurvived new entries	Deaths	Survivors[1] to 1950 (NE)	Net mobility (NM)
(5)	(6)	(7)	(8)	(9)
19.4	222.7	3.7	219.0	+ 260.6
51.8	221.4	3.6	217.8	+ 105.0
11.1	138.8	2.3	136.5	+ 199.0
125.3	286.6	4.6	282.0	+ 6.2
148.9	175.8	2.8	173.0	+ 58.6
93.0	513.3	8.4	504.9	+ 405.0
368.0	871.7	14.2	857.5	+ 69.9
133.4	110.3	1.8	108.5	− 6.5
821.1	196.6	3.2	193.4	− 798.5
368.8	386.9	6.4	380.5	− 299.3
2140.8	3124.1	51.0	3073.1	−

1. Multiplying column (3) and column (6) separately by $.9837 = \dfrac{(.9663)(5213.9)}{(5121.9)}$,
   i.e., product of census survival rate and adjustment factor.

New entries survived to 1940 (NE)	Retirements survived to 1940 (R)	Net mobility (NM)
(5)	(6)	(7)
.2	−	.4
95.0	−	+ 49.9
409.5	−	+ 113.0
386.7	−	+ 91.9
58.3	−	+ 45.0
−	−	+ 12.0
−	−	+ 7.8
−	4.8	− 4.7
−	40.1	− 6.6
−	76.9	+ 1.2
−	129.8	+ 1.6
−	112.8	+ 4.5
−	80.7	−
−	25.3	−
949.7	470.4	+ 315.2

Four sets of projections were made involving assumptions regarding economic conditions during the 1950s and regarding the size of the military in 1960. These projections shown in Table 1 included:

Assuming economic conditions of the 1930s:

A, very few men in the military forces
A', more men in the military forces

Assuming economic conditions of the 1940s:

B, very few men in the military forces
B', more men in the military forces

For all four sets of projections the balancing equation, (1) $O_{1960} = O_{1950} - D + NE - R \pm NM$, was used for each five-year age cohort and major occupational category.

When the components of occupational change in the 1930s and 1940s were being analyzed, net mobility was estimated residually from (1) after all the other terms had been independently estimated. Projection-making proceeds otherwise, we start off with the observed in 1950 as given, estimate deaths, new entries, retirements and net mobility somehow from what they were in the 1930s (or in the 1940s) and then obtain an estimate of the observed in 1960 residually by summing up the terms on the right hand side of (1).

The main methodological problem was how to proceed from estimates of deaths, new entries, retirements and net mobility in the 1930s and in the 1940s to estimates of deaths, new entries, retirements and net mobility in the 1950s. With the exception of deaths, estimates of these components were expressed as rates of change and then these rates were applied to the 1950 observed (i.e., census) data. What kinds of rates were used and how they were used will be the subject of most of this chapter.

Rates of Change For Each of the Components

Following are described the procedures whereby rates of change useful for projection purposes were calculated. These rates were applied to the 1950 census enumeration to produce the two basic projections, i.e., that utilizing the rates of the 1930s and that utilizing the rates of the 1940s. These basic projections were then modified to permit variations in the size of the military. The detailed procedures for the projections and the adjustments necessary to allow for variations in the size of the armed forces are shown in the following section.

Deaths. Deaths were estimated by census survival rates just as in the 1930s and the 1940s. Ten-year census survival rates were computed from Census Bureau population projections to 1960 in which estimates of the male population by five-year age groups are given as of July 1, 1950, and July 1, 1960. Table 26 gives these census survival rates and describes how they were computed.

New entries. New entry rates for the 1930s and 1940s were computed, as illustrated in Table 27, as the ratio of survived intercensal new entries in each occupation to the total survivors of those not in the working force at the beginning of the decade. These are true rates, being the proportion of all those exposed to the probability of entering who actually did enter.

Occupational rates of increase by virtue of new entries (i.e., each row of column (3) divided by the corresponding row of column (2)) were also considered and rejected, mainly because of their unrealiability when applied to the younger ages. Even the cohort age 15 to 19 (Table 27) has extremely large rates of increase for some

TABLE 26
CENSUS SURVIVAL RATES, 1950-60

Age at beginning of decade	Ten-year census survival rate[1]
5 - 9	1.0041
10 - 14	1.0046
15 - 19	1.0072
20 - 24	1.0066
25 - 29	1.0017
30 - 34	.9919
35 - 39	.9723
40 - 44	.9395
45 - 49	.8927
50 - 54	.8350
55 - 59	.7534
60 - 64	.6544

Source: U. S. Bureau of the Census: Current Population Reports, Series P-25, No. 78.

1. Computed by dividing estimated population in age group as of July 1, 1960, by estimated population in age group ten years younger as of July 1, 1950, e.g., 5,401 thousands (estimated population 45 to 49 in 1960) divided by 5,555 (estimated population 35 to 39 in 1950) equals .9723.

TABLE 27
COMPUTATION OF NEW ENTRY RATES INTO MALE WORKING FORCE, 1940-50
COHORT AGE 15 TO 19 IN 1940
(Numbers in thousands)

Occupation	Observed in 1940 Survived to 1950	New entries survived to 1950	New entry rate
(1)	(2)	(3)	(4)
Professional, technical and kindred workers	19.4	219.0	.0572
Farmers and farm managers	51.8	217.8	.0568
Managers, officials and proprietors, except farm	11.1	136.5	.0356
Clerical and kindred workers	125.3	282.0	.0736
Sales workers	148.9	173.0	.0452
Craftsmen, foremen and kindred workers	93.0	504.9	.1318
Operatives and kindred workers	368.0	857.5	.2238
Service workers	133.4	108.5	.0283
Farm laborers and foremen	821.1	193.4	.0505
Laborers except farm and mine	368.8	380.5	.0993
All occupations	2140.8	3073.1	.8021
Total population	5972.1	-	-
Not in working force	3831.3	-	-

occupations. These rates become fantastically large for the cohort age 10 to 14 so that any fluctuations in working force participation at age 14 would result in greatly magnified estimates of new entries in the 1950s.

Retirements. Retirement rates were computed (see Table 28) as the proportion of the observed in each occupation at the beginning of the decade and surviving to the end of the decade who actually did retire, i.e., the number of survived and retired out of all those in the occupation at the beginning of the decade and surviving to the end.

Net mobility. No net mobility rates could be devised which would be completely satisfactory in the sense that when applied to age cohorts with a different occupational distribution would: (a) always have total net in-mobility equal to total net out-mobility, (b) never have more out-mobility from an occupation than were in the occupation to begin with, and (c) never have astronomically large in-mobility.

The rates finally adopted, after careful consideration of many alternatives, satisfy only the last two of these requirements. They are, however, true rates in the sense of signifying the proportion moving of all those who could have moved. The net out-mobility rate for an occupation was taken as the ratio of those who moved out of an occupation to the number expected at the end of the decade under the assumption of no net mobility, i.e., to the survivors of the observed at the beginning of the decade plus the surviving new entries in the occupation (or minus the surviving retired from the occupation).

The net in-mobility rate was figured somewhat differently. All those who could have moved (net movement) into an occupation is the sum of the expected at the end of the decade in all the occupations combined which experienced net out-mobility. As illustrated in Table 29, the net in-mobility was therefore the ratio of those who did move into an occupation to the sum of those who were in all the occupations having out-mobility and who survived to the end of the decade.

The appropriateness of rates of this kind for measuring net out and net in-mobility requires investigation. Total net out-mobility will not ordinarily equal net in-mobility when the rates computed as described above on the basis of one occupational distribution are then applied to a different occupational distribution. However, occupational mobility refers to movement out from one occupation and into another so that there can be no in-mobility without an accompanying out-mobility, and vice versa. Consequently final estimates of total net out-mobility must be exactly equal to total net in-mobility. If the rates selected do not achieve this result, then some kind of adjustment will have to be made. Other things being equal, it is clearly preferable to work with rates which yield estimates that do not require adjustment.

Other rates can be devised whereby estimates of total net in- and total out-mobility will always be at the same level. Each of those examined, however, had other more serious limitations which would in the last analysis require adjustments both more drastic and more arbitrary than those we actually had to employ. These rejected procedures are briefly described as follows.

1. One rate examined in this connection was the amount of intercensal net mobility (whether in or out) in each occupation, divided by the expected total number of the age cohort in the entire working force at the end of the decade. The sum of the out-mobility rates would be equal to the sum of the in-mobility rates; estimating net mobility for a subsequent cohort would be done by multiplying each rate by the expected total number in the working force of the subsequent cohort at the end of the decade; hence the volume of net in-mobility and of net out-mobility must necessarily be equal.

But this rate leaves out of consideration altogether the size of the occupations experiencing a given amount of net mobility. If an occupation should have a

TABLE 28
COMPUTATION OF RETIREMENT RATES FROM MALE WORKING FORCE, 1940-50
COHORT AGE 50 TO 54 IN 1940
(Numbers in thousands)

Occupation	Observed in 1940 survived to 1950	Retirement survived to 1950	Retirement[1] rate
(1)	(2)	(3)	(4)
Professional, technical and kindred workers	141.7	9.5	.0670
Farmers and farm managers	475.0	85.2	.1794
Managers, officials and proprietors, except farm	333.7	43.2	.1295
Clerical and kindred workers	121.5	4.7	.0387
Sales workers	143.3	10.9	.0761
Craftsmen, foremen and kindred workers	522.3	39.3	.0752
Operatives and kindred workers	382.5	27.5	.0719
Service workers	181.0	.8	.0044
Farm laborers and foremen	101.0	18.2	.1802
Laborers except farm and mine	301.6	65.1	.2158
All occupations	2703.6	304.4	.1126

1. Dividing each entry in column (3) by corresponding entry in column (2).

TABLE 29
COMPUTATION OF NET MOBILITY RATES FOR MALE WORKING FORCE, 1940-50
COHORT AGE 15 TO 19 IN 1940
(Numbers in thousands)

Occupation	Expected 1950[1] (adjusted)	Exposed to[2] net mobility	Net[3] mobility	Net mobility rate
(1)	(2)	(3)	(4)	(5)
Professional, technical and kindred workers	238.4	2005.7	+ 260.6	+ .1299
Farmers and farm managers	269.6	2005.7	+ 105.0	+ .0524
Managers, officials and proprietors, except farm	147.6	2005.7	+ 199.0	+ .0992
Clerical and kindred workers	407.3	2005.7	+ 6.2	+ .0031
Sales workers	321.9	2005.7	+ 58.6	+ .0292
Craftsmen, foremen and kindred workers	597.9	2005.7	+ 405.0	+ .2019
Operatives and kindred workers	1225.5	2005.7	+ 69.9	+ .0349
Service workers	241.9	241.9	- 6.5	- .0269
Farm laborers and foremen	1014.5	1014.5	- 798.5	- .7871
Laborers except farm and mine	749.3	749.3	- 299.3	- .3994
All occupations	5213.9	-	± 1104.3	+ .5506

1. See Tables 21 to 23 and accompanying text for meaning of expected end of decade (adjusted).

2. For each occupation having net out-mobility in column (4) this entry is identical with column (2), i.e., the number who could have moved out of the occupation; for each occupation having net in-mobility in column (4) this entry is the sum of expected 1950 (adjusted) of those occupations having net out-mobility, i.e., those who could have moved into the occupation given the net trends observed in the decade.

3. Each entry of column (4) divided by corresponding entry of column (3). The value +.5506 equals the sum of all the plus (+) rates.

considerably smaller number of persons in it in 1950, say, than it had in 1940, then we should want to attribute to it a smaller volume of out-migration in the 1950s than it had in the 1940s. Yet, with this rate - since the size of the working force for all age groups is larger in the 1950s than in the 1940s - the estimated volume of net out-mobility could be larger than the numbers in the occupation. It is clear that a realistic out-mobility must be related to the size of the occupation.

2. Another rate considered would have related volume of mobility experienced by each occupation to the sum of the out-mobility occupations of the expected at the end of the decade. In-mobility rates by this standard would be the same as those finally adopted, while out-mobility rates would be related to all the out-mobility occupations rather than to each one separately. In this instance estimated net out-mobility is related to the size of all the out-mobility occupations and therefore is not completely insensitive to changes in the size of the out-mobility occupations. On the other hand, the estimated volume of total net out-mobility will always match the total volume of net in-mobility. This is so because all the occupational mobility rates are multiplied by the same numerical value, i.e., the number of persons expected at the end of the decade in all of the occupations which experienced out-mobility in the preceding decade. Yet even this rate is unsatisfactory by comparison with the one we selected because absurd estimates of net out-mobility (more than were in the occupation at the beginning of the decade) sometimes result.

3. A third alternative to the type of rate we chose to use would eliminate the difficulty just mentioned by working with rates of increase or decrease accruing to each occupation because of net mobility. In this way, the net out-mobility rate would be the same as the one we adopted (i.e., amount of out-mobility in an occupation divided by the expected number in the occupation) so that the volume of estimated out-mobility would decrease with decreasing size of an occupation. The trouble here is that the volume of in-mobility would be increasing at the same time with increasing size of occupation with the result that the difference between estimated total net in- and total net out-mobility becomes large.

The procedures we finally decided upon and which are shown in Table 29 have two advantages: (a) Occupations which have experienced net out-mobility in the past of necessity must have a smaller volume of net out-mobility in the future. The size of these occupations which are losing workers can approach but never reach zero. Since the volume of net out-mobility is decreasing, the volume of net in-mobility also must decrease. The occupations which experienced net in-mobility in the past will continue to gain via mobility in the future, but only by an amount approximately equal to the amount lost by those occupations which had out-mobility.

These procedures also supply a measure of the level of total mobility in a past decade which can be used as a guide for adjusting the projections. The level of total mobility in a past decade can be calculated as the ratio of the sum of either the in-mobility or the out-mobility to the sum of the total expected in the out-mobility occupations. This is quantitatively equivalent to the sum of the net in-mobility rates (.5506 in Table 29). Consequently when we assume that the cohort age 15 to 19 in 1950 has the same net mobility experience in the 1950s as the cohort of similar age in 1940 had in the 1940s, we want and in fact are able with these rates to attribute the same level of mobility to the subsequent cohort. As we shall see, total net in-mobility is set at the required level so that it is out-mobility which has to be adjusted in order for total out-mobility to equal total in-mobility. Furthermore as it works out arithmetically, estimated out-mobility is generally less than estimated in-mobility, and an analysis of the reason for this affords us some sort of rational basis for determining what kind of adjustment of estimated out-mobility is most suitable.

Estimated net out-mobility will generally be less than estimated net in-mobility because the occupations with the highest out-mobility rates and which proportionately contributed the most out-mobility (e.g., farm laborers and foremen in the 1940s in Table 29), precisely because of their out-mobility losses, are no longer capable of losing as much as the other out-mobility occupations. On the other hand, the occupations with low out-mobility rates in the past will come to constitute a more significant part of the out-mobility occupations and will therefore be relatively more able to contribute more workers to the in-mobility occupations. Out-mobility was adjusted upwards in these occupations in accordance with their expected size in 1960. Precise details of this adjustment can be described most easily through a concrete example. So let us now turn to the application of the rates of the components of occupational change and consider the computations involved in the construction of the projections.

The Projection Calculations

Deaths. Table 30 traces through all the computations involved in projecting the cohort age 15 to 19 in 1950 as observed in 1950 to its estimated 1960 occupational distribution under the assumption that its experience will parallel that experienced by the corresponding cohort in the 1940s. Deaths (and net immigration, faulty age-reporting, etc.) were allowed for by applying the appropriate census survival rate of Table 26 to the observed in 1950; thus we obtain in column (3) the numbers of survivors by occupation estimated for 1960.

New entries. Footnote 2 (Table 30) is virtually self-explanatory. To estimate the number of surviving new entries for each occupation, each occupational new entry rate for the 1940s was multiplied by the number of those who could have entered the occupation as a new entry, i.e., all those not in the labor force in 1960 if there had been no intercensal new entries. The expected in 1960 under the assumption of no net mobility is the sum of the surviving new entries in column (4) and the survivors of the observed in 1950 in column (3).

Retirements. Retirements were not estimated in Table 30 because the cohort age 15 to 19 in 1950 was too young to be exposed to retirements. In the case of cohorts exposed to retirements, such as the cohort 50 to 54 shown in Table 28, the observed in 1950 were survived to 1960 exactly as in Table 30; then the number of survived retirements were estimated by the product of each occupational retirement rate and the number of estimated survivors in the occupation. The expected in 1960 under the assumption of no net mobility was obtained by subtracting the survived and retired from the survivors of the observed in 1950.

Net mobility. Since net mobility rates were calculated on the basis of the volume of net mobility relative to the expected at the end of the decade (Table 29), net mobility to 1960 was estimated from the expected in 1960 and the net mobility rates of either the 1930s or the 1940s. In Table 30 those exposed to net mobility in column (6) were obtained from the expected in column (5); those exposed to net in-mobility are the sum of the out-mobility occupations in column (5). The occupations having net out-mobility were of course the same as in the 1940s since the net mobility rates of that decade were being projected.

As was anticipated, the net mobility estimates in column (7), computed as the product of each row of column (5) in Table 29 by the corresponding row of column (6), reveal an excess of net in-mobility over net out-mobility. Out-mobility had to be adjusted because we wished the level of total mobility to be the same as in the 1940s, .5506, in this case, or 907.9 thousands divided by 1649.0 thousands.

Net out-mobility among service workers and laborers except farm and mine was adjusted upward because in 1960 the workers in these two occupations comprised a larger proportion of the workers in all out-mobility occupations than they had in 1950. Of the three out-mobility occupations in expected at end of decade, service workers and laborers except farm and mine were 16.0 percent and 38.4 percent respectively in 1960 as compared

TABLE 30
1960 PROJECTION COMPUTATIONS
(BASED ON EXPERIENCE OF 1940s)
FOR MALE WORKING FORCE
COHORT AGE 15 TO 19 IN 1960
(Number in thousands)

Occupation	Observed in 1950	Survivors[1] to 1960	New entries to 196
(1)	(2)	(3)	(4)
Professional, technical and kindred workers	37.3	37.6	181.0
Farmers and farm managers	65.5	66.0	179.8
Managers, officials and proprietors, except farm	20.3	20.4	112.7
Clerical and kindred workers	157.0	158.1	232.9
Sales workers	208.9	210.4	143.1
Craftsmen, foremen and kindred workers	137.9	138.9	417.2
Operatives and kindred workers	464.6	468.0	708.3
Service workers	173.0	174.2	89.6
Farm laborers and foremen	588.6	592.9	159.8
Laborers except farm and mine	315.9	318.2	314.3
All occupations	2169.0	2184.7	2538.7
Total population	5311.3	5349.8	-
Not in working force	-	3165.1	-

1. Multiplying column (2) by census survival rate of 1.0072.
2. Multiplying survivors not in working force (i.e., 3165.1) by new entry rates of
        Table 27, column (4).
3. Column (3) plus column (4).
4. See footnote 2, Table 29. Out-mobility occupations are assumed to be the same as in
        1940-49.
5. Multiplying each row of column (6) by corresponding row of column (5) in Table 29.

TABLE 31
MALE WORKING FORCE PARTICIPATION RATES,[1] BY AGE, 1930, 1940, 1950 AND 1960
(1960 unadjusted for military)

Age	1930	1940	1950
15 - 19	47.5	35.2	40.8
20 - 24	89.0	83.9	76.0
25 - 29	96.4	93.6	87.3
30 - 34	97.3	95.0	91.3
35 - 39	97.5	95.1	93.9
40 - 44	97.5	94.3	93.4
45 - 49	97.1	92.7	93.2
50 - 54	95.6	91.0	90.1
55 - 59	93.0	87.7	87.1
60 - 64	86.7	79.2	79.0
65 - 69	75.7	59.7	61.1
70 - 74	57.5	37.6	37.1

1. Rate expressed as percentage of male population in the working force.

Expected 1960[3]	Exposed to[4] net mobility	Net mobility[5]	Allocation of[6] out-mobility deficiency	Net mobility[7] (adjusted)	Estimated[8] 1960
(5)	(6)	(7)	(8)	(9)	(10)
218.6	1649.0	+ 214.2	-	+ 214.2	432.8
245.8	1649.0	+ 86.4	-	+ 86.4	332.2
133.1	1649.0	+ 163.6	-	+ 163.6	296.7
391.0	1649.0	+ 5.1	-	+ 5.1	396.1
353.5	1649.0	+ 48.2	-	+ 48.2	401.7
556.1	1649.0	+ 332.9	-	+ 332.9	889.0
1176.3	1649.0	+ 57.5	-	+ 57.5	1233.8
263.8	263.8	- 7.1	- 16.4	- 23.5	240.3
752.7	752.7	- 592.5	-	- 592.5	160.2
632.5	632.5	- 252.6	- 39.3	- 291.9	340.6
4723.4	-	(+ 907.9	-	± 907.9	4723.4
-	-	(- 852.2	-	-	5349.8
-			-		

6. Deficiency of out-mobility of 55.7 (907.9-852.2); 29.4 percent and 70.6 percent
   respectively allocated to service workers and other laborers on basis of
   their relative expected size in 1960 (column (5); allocated to these two
   occupations because their size in expected 1960 relative to all out-mobility
   occupations was larger than for expected 1950.
7. Column (7) plus column (8).
8. Column (5) plus column (9).

	1960	
Based on 1930's experience		Based on 1940's experience
35.2		40.8
84.0		76.3
92.8		88.3
80.8		79.8
87.3		87.3
91.3		91.3
93.9		93.9
91.8		92.1
86.0		90.9
74.7		81.0
54.0		59.7
33.5		37.6

with 12.1 percent and 37.3 percent in 1950. In column (8) the out-mobility deficiency of 55.7 thousands was allocated 29.4 percent to service workers and 70.6 percent to other laborers on the basis of their respective sizes in 1960.

Adjusted net mobility was obtained in column (8) by adding the allocated deficiency in column (7) to the unadjusted net mobility of column (7). Finally we estimate the distribution of the cohort in 1960 by summing net mobility in column (9) and 1960 expected under the assumption of no net mobility, column (5).

Age Group Projections Revised

The preceding calculations resulted in 1960 projections which were based on the age and occupational composition of the male civilian working force as observed by the United States Census of Population in 1950. It is clear, however, that the unadjusted results of such straightforward projections cannot be used because of complications introduced by the military.

Comparing working force participation rates by age for each set of projections with similar rates by age as of 1930, 1940 and 1950 (see Table 31) brings out rather clearly, with the exception of the younger ages, the over-all accuracy of the projections with reference to participation in the working force. When the younger age groups are examined more closely, it is quickly seen that discrepancies with past performance can mainly be attributed to the changing size of the military at each time period as well as to the differential participation of various age groups in the armed forces.

Cohorts age 30 to 34, 35 to 39 and 40 to 44 in 1960 are all underestimated in 1960 because large numbers of them were in the armed forces in 1950; up to this point our model for estimating intercensal new entries makes no provision for re-entering into the civilian working force those who had temporarily withdrawn into military service. Indeed this was no problem in either of the past two decades when the size of the armed forces was relatively small at the beginning of the decade. Re-entries into the civilian working force by those who were in the armed forces at the beginning of the decade was an insignificant factor in the past two decades. Assuming that the 1950s will parallel the experience of either the 1930s or the 1940s therefore implicitly carries with it the assumption that such re-entries will also be insignificant in the 1960s when in fact they cannot be insignificant.

In 1950 age groups 20 to 24, 25 to 29 and 30 to 34 all under-participated in the civilian working force either because of service in the armed forces or because of deferred re-entry into the civilian working force due to veteran status under the GI Bill of Rights. Accordingly the 1960 projections for these age cohorts had to be adjusted to allow for the re-entry of these men by 1960. Other adjustments had to be made for the groups under age 30 in 1960 before the four series, A, A', B and B' could be obtained.

Cohort Age 15 to 19 in 1960. A straightforward projection of the 1950 data for this cohort begins with the children aged 5 to 9 in 1950. When we apply the various component rates by the 1930s to this cohort, we estimate a situation with few men in the military forces in 1960. This follows since there were few men aged 15 to 19 in the military forces in 1940. Hence this projection is the A projection.

To obtain the A' projection, it is necessary to subtract off the estimated number who might be in the armed forces. In 1950 there were 213,000 men aged 15 to 19 in the armed forces stationed in the United States; this number was subtracted off. In order to estimate the numbers in each occupation, these 213,000 were assumed to have the same occupational distribution as in the A projection.

A straightforward projection of the cohort age 5 to 9 in 1950, using the component rates of the 1940s, provides the B' estimate. This is because withdrawals to the to the military have been built into these rates since the rates represent the actual experience in the 1940s of a similarly aged cohort. To obtain the B projection, we add in 213,000 men; this is the reverse of the procedures whereby the A projection was converted into the A' estimate.

Cohort age 20 to 24 in 1960. This age cohort was handled in exactly the same way as the preceding age group. In this case about 309,000 men were subtracted off, or added in, as the case may be.

Cohort age 25 to 29 in 1960. The procedures here are the same as for the preceding cohorts. For this group the men in the armed forces who were stationed in the United States in 1950, and who were either subtracted off or added in, numbered 178,000.

Cohort age 30 to 34 in 1960. With either set of projections this cohort was estimated to have a civilian working force participation rate of about 80.0 in 1960 - a figure substantially under that achieved by the corresponding age groups in the past three censuses. Its low civilian working force participation rate of 76.0 in 1950, when it was age 20 to 24, plus an analysis of those not in the working force at that time (390 thousand in the armed forces; 625 thousand in school) clearly indicated that an adjustment for re-entries should be made. The assumption was made that the 1950 pre-Korean military situation would prevail in 1960 and that therefore this cohort would have the same civilian working force participation rate in 1960 (91.3) as that of the age group 30 to 34 in 1950. The occupational distribution of the re-entries necessary to raise the participation rate to this level not being known, it was decided to allocate them according to the occupational distribution of similarly aged intercensal new entries in the 1930s and 1940s respectively for each set of projections. These procedures obviously result in the same military levels as were reported in 1950 for all four projections.

Cohort age 35 to 39 in 1960. By the same line of reasoning it was decided to adjust this cohort's estimated 1960 civilian working force participation from 87.3 to 93.9 (i.e., equal to the age group 35 to 39 in 1950) and hence to re-enter 394.6 thousand workers. Of these 238.9 thousands were the expected survivors of those in school in 1950; they were brought into the working force with the same occupational distribution as new entries age 25 to 29 in the pre-censal year of 1949. The occupational distribution of the resulting revised 1960 estimate was used as the basis for allocating the balance of 155.7 thousands required to get a working force participation rate of 93.9.

Cohort age 40 to 44 in 1960. About 116.6 thousand re-entries were needed to raise the estimated 1960 civilian working force participation rate of this cohort to the 93.4 achieved by the age group 40 to 44 in 1950. In 1950 there were some 136.0 thousands in the armed forces, while numbers in school were not tabulated - presumably because insignificant. Accordingly all 116.6 thousands re-entries were allocated to the civilian working force in accordance with the occupational distribution of the unadjusted 1960 estimates.

Cohort age 45 and over in 1960. The 1960 projections for these ages were not adjusted in any way. Hence they contain the same levels of military forces as they had in 1950, when they were age 35 and over.

CHAPTER 16
COMPARISON OF THE METHODOLOGY OF
THE SIX CITY STUDY WITH THIS STUDY

It would seem that the detailed findings on mobility from our study can be compared with the findings of the Six City Study only with difficulty, if at all. This is due to the fact that the two studies were conducted in such entirely different ways and include different universes. Some of the differences are as follows.[1]

Universe. Our study includes the total United States. The Six City Study includes only six cities; workers in all rural areas were excluded. Furthermore these cities were not necessarily a correct sample of the entire country. With respect to the persons covered, we considered all men in the United States, including those in and out of the working force. The Six City Study was limited to persons who were employed in 1950.

Coverage. Our study includes 100 percent coverage of the earlier censuses and 3-1/3 percent coverage of the 1950 census returns. The Six City Study contained about 9,000 cases of men all told; accordingly each cell contains a considerably larger sampling variability than a corresponding cell from our study would have.

Occupational distribution. For some reason the Six City Study did not locate many men who claimed to have been farm laborers in 1940. Yet there appears to have been a very great deal of out-mobility from this occupation during the 1940s. Our study took such out-mobility into account with consequent effects upon the mobility rates of all other occupations.

Method of observation. The Six City Study interviewed the persons and obtained their work histories from 1940 to 1950. Thus the actual changes which took place were recorded, subject to any limitations of the respondents' memories. Our study, on the other hand, was based on decennial population census data and inferred the changes which occurred. Thus we could compute only net changes whereas the Six City Study could note gross changes.

Notwithstanding these and other differences it is believed the major generalized findings of the two studies are in reasonably close agreement. For example, we noted in Table 9 that the patterns of mobility by age were shown to be substantially the same by both studies.

Furthermore the direction of net mobility by occupation was shown to be the same in both studies, for all eight nonagricultural occupation groups. Both studies showed four to have net in-mobility:

    Professional, technical and kindred workers
    Managers, officials and proprietors, except farm
    Craftsmen, foremen and kindred workers
    Service workers

The remaining four occupations were shown to have experienced net out-mobility during the 1940s.

Attempts were made to compare the rates of new entries by occupation in the two studies. Because of the intrinsic differences in the methodologies, however, this could not be done.

---

1. For a detailed description of the methods used in the Six City Study, see Appendix B, "Technical Notes," of that volume.

In summary it should be remembered that the Six City Study was designed to investigate many aspects of labor mobility other than occupational. Hence most of the subject matter of these two studies do not overlap; one should not necessarily expect to find either agreements or disagreements in results of the two studies.

APPENDIX TABLE 1
MALE WORKING FORCE BY AGE AND
OCCUPATION, 1930, 1940, 1950
AND 1960
(Numbers in thousands)

Professional, technical and kindred workers

1930 Age	No.	1940 Age	No.	1950 Age	No.	1960 Age	A	B	A'	B'
-	-	-	-	-	-	15-19	21.6	52.3	19.7	48.5
-	-	-	-	-	-	20-24	186.1	259.7	174.1	242.4
-	-	-	-	15-19	37.3	25-29	350.4	449.2	337.8	432.8
-	-	-	-	20-24	236.6	30-34	453.4	542.0	453.4	542.0
-	-	15-19	19.7	25-29	499.0	35-39	635.0	620.5	635.0	620.5
-	-	20-24	183.6	30-34	460.2	40-44	498.6	485.1	498.6	485.1
15-19	28.4	25-29	355.2	35-39	427.8	45-49	445.1	423.3	445.1	423.3
20-24	185.5	30-34	380.2	40-44	392.1	50-54	384.8	387.6	384.8	387.6
25-29	271.8	35-39	327.5	45-49	312.9	55-59	275.8	295.4	275.8	295.4
30-34	248.7	40-44	258.6	50-54	252.8	60-64	196.7	204.2	196.7	204.2
35-39	229.0	45-49	217.8	55-59	198.1	65-69	111.2	109.2	111.2	109.2
40-44	193.1	50-54	178.9	60-64	139.0	70-74	54.4	53.4	54.4	53.4
45-49	162.4	55-59	131.3	65-69	80.5	-	-	-	-	-
50-54	139.7	60-64	98.8	70-74	39.7	-	-	-	-	-
55-59	104.7	65-69	61.0	-	-	-	-	-	-	-
60-64	76.4	70-74	30.1	-	-	-	-	-	-	-
65-69	44.8	-	-	-	-	-	-	-	-	-
70-74	24.9	-	-	-	-	-	-	-	-	-
Total	1709.4	Total	2242.7	Total	3076.0	Total	3613.1	3881.9	3586.6	3844.4

Managers, officials and proprietors, except farm

1930 Age	No.	1940 Age	No.	1950 Age	No.	1960 Age	A	B	A'	B'
-	-	-	-	-	-	15-19	12.1	26.9	11.0	25.0
-	-	-	-	-	-	20-24	115.4	151.9	108.0	141.7
-	-	-	-	15-19	20.3	25-29	267.4	307.9	257.8	296.7
-	-	-	-	20-24	139.6	30-34	376.4	505.5	376.4	505.5
-	-	15-19	11.3	25-29	346.6	35-39	586.1	708.9	586.1	708.9
-	-	20-24	115.5	30-34	498.2	40-44	601.8	751.2	601.8	751.2
15-19	23.8	25-29	283.2	35-39	607.0	45-49	613.6	779.6	613.6	779.6
20-24	166.8	30-34	394.5	40-44	637.9	50-54	558.7	688.3	558.7	688.3
25-29	324.7	35-39	457.3	45-49	599.6	55-59	465.7	571.0	465.7	571.0
30-34	448.1	40-44	497.7	50-54	535.3	60-64	338.9	398.0	338.9	398.0
35-39	546.8	45-49	483.9	55-59	440.5	65-69	192.5	225.8	192.5	225.8
40-44	523.3	50-54	421.3	60-64	298.8	70-74	101.1	96.9	101.1	96.9
45-49	461.6	55-59	318.8	65-69	172.5	-	-	-	-	-
50-54	391.7	60-64	226.8	70-74	76.8	-	-	-	-	-
55-59	290.9	65-69	129.9	-	-	-	-	-	-	-
60-64	208.7	70-74	70.8	-	-	-	-	-	-	-
65-69	123.4	-	-	-	-	-	-	-	-	-
70-74	60.7	-	-	-	-	-	-	-	-	-
Total	3570.5	Total	3411.0	Total	4373.1	Total	4229.7	5211.9	4211.6	5188.6

Farmers and farm managers

1930		1940		1950		1960				
Age	No.	Age	No.	Age	No.	Age	A	B	A'	B'
-	-	-	-	-	-	15-19	57.3	88.0	52.2	81.6
-	-	-	-	-	-	20-24	303.7	249.5	284.0	232.8
-	-	-	-	15-19	65.5	25-29	474.2	344.7	457.1	332.2
-	-	-	-	20-24	229.0	30-34	456.5	393.2	456.5	393.2
-	-	15-19	52.6	25-29	374.6	35-39	488.3	444.2	488.3	444.2
-	-	20-24	303.3	30-34	433.0	40-44	470.4	431.3	470.4	431.3
15-19	48.5	25-29	455.8	35-39	488.7	45-49	482.1	441.8	482.1	441.8
20-24	340.6	30-34	503.3	40-44	485.6	50-54	463.1	393.3	463.1	393.3
25-29	491.0	35-39	534.0	45-49	464.3	55-59	387.6	357.3	387.6	357.3
30-34	567.7	40-44	563.1	50-54	440.2	60-64	307.7	283.4	307.7	283.4
35-39	682.5	45-49	599.2	55-59	431.7	65-69	250.0	223.3	250.0	223.3
40-44	673.8	50-54	599.8	60-64	366.2	70-74	152.3	125.9	152.3	125.9
45-49	679.9	55-59	530.5	65-69	285.0	-	-	-	-	-
50-54	653.8	60-64	443.3	70-74	158.4	-	-	-	-	-
55-59	542.1	65-69	323.6	-	-	-	-	-	-	-
60-64	438.9	70-74	183.2	-	-	-	-	-	-	-
65-69	311.5	-	-	-	-	-	-	-	-	-
70-74	196.7	-	-	-	-	-	-	-	-	-
Total	5627.0	Total	5091.7	Total	4222.2	Total	4293.2	3775.9	4251.3	3740.3

Clerical and kindred workers

1930		1940		1950		1960				
Age	No.	Age	No.	Age	No.	Age	A	B	A'	B'
-	-	-	-	-	-	15-19	139.6	210.6	127.0	195.5
-	-	-	-	-	-	20-24	390.6	428.3	365.3	399.9
-	-	-	-	15-19	157.0	25-29	296.2	411.1	285.5	396.1
-	-	-	-	20-24	398.5	30-34	302.5	334.6	302.5	334.6
-	-	15-19	127.4	25-29	413.5	35-39	320.0	308.1	320.0	308.1
-	-	20-24	395.4	30-34	349.9	40-44	314.5	286.5	314.5	286.5
15-19	249.3	25-29	374.4	35-39	304.2	45-49	307.0	282.8	307.0	282.8
20-24	413.2	30-34	318.5	40-44	266.4	50-54	258.7	263.2	258.7	263.2
25-29	323.2	35-39	253.1	45-49	235.8	55-59	197.2	223.7	197.2	223.7
30-34	263.9	40-44	228.1	50-54	219.0	60-64	170.7	189.5	170.7	189.5
35-39	222.1	45-49	197.9	55-59	178.3	65-69	76.9	92.1	76.9	92.1
40-44	170.6	50-54	153.4	60-64	129.6	70-74	27.7	40.3	27.7	40.3
45-49	138.7	55-59	104.9	65-69	69.8	-	-	-	-	-
50-54	112.8	60-64	81.4	70-74	27.7	-	-	-	-	-
55-59	84.1	65-69	38.1	-	-	-	-	-	-	-
60-64	61.1	70-74	13.2	-	-	-	-	-	-	-
65-69	34.1	-	-	-	-	-	-	-	-	-
70-74	15.8	-	-	-	-	-	-	-	-	-
Total	2088.9	Total	2285.8	Total	2749.7	Total	2801.6	3070.8	2753.0	3012.3

MALE WORKING FORCE BY AGE AND OCCUPATION, 1930, 1940, 1950 AND 1960
(Numbers in thousands)

Sales Workers

1930 Age	No.	1940 Age	No.	1950 Age	No.	1960 Age	A	B	A'	B'
15-19	149.1	15-19	151.4	15-19	208.9	15-19	164.5	283.3	149.8	263.0
20-24	285.6	20-24	307.9	20-24	291.4	20-24	338.5	347.7	316.6	324.6
25-29	300.4	25-29	335.2	25-29	380.5	25-29	412.6	416.8	397.8	401.7
30-34	295.0	30-34	303.7	30-34	343.4	30-34	355.9	352.7	355.9	352.7
35-39	276.5	35-39	275.4	35-39	318.0	35-39	360.7	347.9	360.7	347.9
40-44	222.4	40-44	256.0	40-44	269.7	40-44	309.7	299.4	309.7	299.4
45-49	187.0	45-49	225.0	45-49	241.0	45-49	285.9	276.8	285.9	276.8
50-54	151.6	50-54	180.9	50-54	210.7	50-54	238.6	222.4	238.6	222.4
55-59	111.4	55-59	132.5	55-59	166.5	55-59	192.0	184.9	192.0	184.9
60-64	79.3	60-64	89.8	60-64	127.9	60-64	139.1	155.1	139.1	155.1
65-69	47.5	65-69	49.9	65-69	81.1	65-69	73.1	97.0	73.1	97.0
70-74	24.8	70-74	25.0	70-74	34.3	70-74	40.1	46.7	40.1	46.7
Total	2130.6	Total	2332.7	Total	2673.4	Total	2910.7	3030.7	2859.3	2972.2

Operatives and kindred workers

1930 Age	No.	1940 Age	No.	1950 Age	No.	1960 Age	A	B	A'	B'
15-19	520.9	15-19	374.1	15-19	464.6	15-19	408.6	622.0	371.9	577.2
20-24	947.1	20-24	1162.3	20-24	1214.9	20-24	1153.9	1310.2	1079.5	1223.2
25-29	905.8	25-29	1238.0	25-29	1295.4	25-29	1238.1	1280.3	1193.7	1233.8
30-34	777.5	30-34	1055.0	30-34	1205.8	30-34	1474.2	1234.8	1474.2	1234.8
35-39	731.0	35-39	867.1	35-39	1154.2	35-39	1249.8	1128.4	1249.8	1128.4
40-44	590.3	40-44	712.2	40-44	941.0	40-44	1150.9	1056.4	1150.9	1056.4
45-49	468.8	45-49	612.4	45-49	770.0	45-49	1069.2	1020.4	1069.2	1020.4
50-54	345.0	50-54	483.0	50-54	616.8	50-54	837.7	818.1	837.7	818.1
55-59	231.5	55-59	330.8	55-59	500.1	55-59	610.8	653.6	610.8	653.6
60-64	153.9	60-64	203.0	60-64	350.4	60-64	396.8	466.3	396.8	466.3
65-69	87.2	65-69	95.8	65-69	169.9	65-69	203.4	244.3	203.4	244.3
70-74	36.8	70-74	31.9	70-74	54.0	70-74	71.8	88.3	71.8	88.3
Total	5795.8	Total	7165.6	Total	8737.1	Total	9865.2	9923.1	9709.7	9744.8

Craftsmen, foremen and kindred workers

1930 Age	1930 No.	1940 Age	1940 No.	1950 Age	1950 No.	1960 Age	A	B	A'	B'
-	-	-	-	-	-	15-19	103.8	182.2	94.4	169.2
-	-	-	-	-	-	20-24	457.6	704.4	428.0	657.8
-	-	-	-	15-19	137.9	25-29	657.1	922.5	633.6	889.0
-	-	-	-	20-24	652.7	30-34	879.7	1266.4	879.7	1266.4
-	-	15-19	94.6	25-29	1002.9	35-39	1152.1	1483.7	1152.1	1483.7
-	-	20-24	459.5	30-34	1058.0	40-44	1088.4	1330.9	1088.4	1330.9
15-19	144.4	25-29	636.8	35-39	1072.1	45-49	1052.4	1202.6	1052.4	1202.6
20-24	633.6	30-34	751.0	40-44	1000.0	50-54	916.8	1023.4	916.8	1023.4
25-29	791.4	35-39	806.9	45-49	899.9	55-59	728.6	825.1	728.6	825.1
30-34	820.6	40-44	781.3	50-54	788.3	60-64	531.8	599.7	531.8	599.7
35-39	870.3	45-49	749.0	55-59	649.7	65-69	272.4	315.3	272.4	315.3
40-44	782.6	50-54	659.5	60-64	481.4	70-74	99.9	121.3	99.9	121.3
45-49	670.4	55-59	482.7	65-69	246.5	-	-	-	-	-
50-54	529.7	60-64	320.7	70-74	84.9	-	-	-	-	-
55-59	384.1	65-69	164.5	-	-	-	-	-	-	-
60-64	272.9	70-74	56.9	-	-	-	-	-	-	-
65-69	158.2	-	-	-	-	-	-	-	-	-
70-74	70.1	-	-	-	-	-	-	-	-	-
Total	6128.3	Total	5963.4	Total	8074.3	Total	7940.6	9977.5	7878.1	9884.4

Service workers

1930 Age	1930 No.	1940 Age	1940 No.	1950 Age	1950 No.	1960 Age	A	B	A'	B'
-	-	-	-	-	-	15-19	145.7	234.7	132.5	217.8
-	-	-	-	-	-	20-24	256.3	225.6	239.6	210.8
-	-	-	-	15-19	173.0	25-29	351.9	249.4	339.2	240.3
-	-	-	-	20-24	204.7	30-34	312.1	179.3	312.1	179.3
-	-	15-19	135.6	25-29	235.4	35-39	329.1	243.6	329.1	243.6
-	-	20-24	252.8	30-34	236.2	40-44	327.2	244.9	327.2	244.9
15-19	103.1	25-29	272.3	35-39	263.0	45-49	331.7	267.5	331.7	267.5
20-24	183.2	30-34	262.1	40-44	263.1	50-54	325.1	272.6	325.1	272.6
25-29	212.4	35-39	269.1	45-49	262.3	55-59	282.4	289.3	282.4	289.3
30-34	213.9	40-44	271.1	50-54	269.8	60-64	254.3	268.7	254.3	268.7
35-39	224.3	45-49	250.2	55-59	262.9	65-69	156.7	180.3	156.7	180.3
40-44	197.7	50-54	228.6	60-64	221.5	70-74	81.8	102.2	81.8	102.2
45-49	175.1	55-59	177.8	65-69	151.4	-	-	-	-	-
50-54	154.1	60-64	143.2	70-74	70.9	-	-	-	-	-
55-59	121.2	65-69	87.5	-	-	-	-	-	-	-
60-64	99.6	70-74	38.7	-	-	-	-	-	-	-
65-69	69.6	-	-	-	-	-	-	-	-	-
70-74	37.6	-	-	-	-	-	-	-	-	-
Total	1791.8	Total	2389.0	Total	2614.2	Total	3154.3	2758.1	3111.7	2717.3

Farm laborers and foremen

1930 Age	1930 No.	1940 Age	1940 No.	1950 Age	1950 No.	1960 Age	A	B	A'	B'
-	-	-	-	-	-	15-19	910.2	836.8	828.6	776.7
-	-	-	-	-	-	20-24	741.4	397.9	693.6	371.4
-	-	-	-	15-19	588.6	25-29	299.3	166.3	288.6	160.2
-	-	-	-	20-24	365.8	30-34	131.1	73.4	131.1	73.4
-	-	15-19	834.7	25-29	216.0	35-39	120.5	72.9	120.5	72.9
-	-	20-24	761.3	30-34	151.3	40-44	102.9	70.8	102.9	70.8
15-19	1031.2	25-29	441.7	35-39	146.9	45-49	106.7	81.3	106.7	81.3
20-24	814.0	30-34	274.7	40-44	124.4	50-54	98.8	77.8	98.8	77.8
25-29	407.1	35-39	213.1	45-49	113.4	55-59	89.8	74.2	89.8	74.2
30-34	253.1	40-44	160.8	50-54	97.0	60-64	60.8	62.8	60.8	62.8
35-39	207.9	45-49	135.2	55-59	82.9	65-69	38.3	44.8	38.3	44.8
40-44	170.2	50-54	127.5	60-64	78.3	70-74	15.9	29.2	15.9	29.2
45-49	160.4	55-59	118.9	65-69	65.2	-	-	-	-	-
50-54	144.2	60-64	87.8	70-74	34.0	-	-	-	-	-
55-59	117.0	65-69	64.4	-	-	-	-	-	-	-
60-64	97.9	70-74	12.9	-	-	-	-	-	-	-
65-69	72.8	-	-	-	-	-	-	-	-	-
70-74	44.1	-	-	-	-	-	-	-	-	-
Total	3519.9	Total	3233.0	Total	2063.8	Total	2715.7	1988.2	2575.6	1895.5

All occupations

1930 Age	1930 No.	1940 Age	1940 No.	1950 Age	1950 No.	1960 Age	A	B	A'	B'
-	-	-	-	-	-	15-19	2374.0	2966.8	2160.8	2753.6
-	-	-	-	-	-	20-24	4776.5	4647.3	4468.0	4338.8
-	-	-	-	15-19	2169.0	25-29	4962.7	4901.6	4784.5	4723.4
-	-	-	-	20-24	4261.2	30-34	5152.2	5152.2	5152.2	5152.2
-	-	15-19	2176.3	25-29	5213.9	35-39	5617.1	5617.1	5617.1	5617.1
-	-	20-24	4777.2	30-34	5135.9	40-44	5211.1	5211.1	5211.1	5211.1
15-19	2733.7	25-29	5101.6	35-39	5181.5	45-49	5037.9	5037.9	5037.9	5037.9
20-24	4748.0	30-34	4817.0	40-44	4734.2	50-54	4374.7	4387.9	4374.7	4387.9
25-29	4683.2	35-39	4512.3	45-49	4219.9	55-59	3475.9	3673.5	3475.9	3673.5
30-34	4437.2	40-44	4168.5	50-54	3718.9	60-64	2574.2	2792.6	2574.2	2792.6
35-39	4561.7	45-49	3901.8	55-59	3161.3	65-69	1476.6	1632.6	1476.6	1632.6
40-44	4030.6	50-54	3413.7	60-64	2399.2	70-74	665.7	747.9	665.7	747.9
45-49	3565.3	55-59	2641.0	65-69	1444.6	-	-	-	-	-
50-54	2994.2	60-64	1899.2	70-74	625.6	-	-	-	-	-
55-59	2256.1	65-69	1131.9	-	-	-	-	-	-	-
60-64	1684.5	70-74	477.7	-	-	-	-	-	-	-
65-69	1072.8	-	-	-	-	-	-	-	-	-
70-74	570.2	-	-	-	-	-	-	-	-	-
Total	37337.5	Total	39018.2	Total	42265.2	Total	45698.6	46768.5	44998.7	46068.6

Laborers except farm and mine

1930 Age	1930 No.	1940 Age	1940 No.	1950 Age	1950 No.	1960 Age	A	B	A'	B'
-	-	-	-	-	-	15-19	410.6	430.0	373.7	399.1
-	-	-	-	-	-	20-24	833.0	572.1	779.3	534.2
-	-	-	-	15-19	315.9	25-29	615.5	353.4	593.4	340.6
-	-	-	-	20-24	528.0	30-34	410.4	270.3	410.4	270.3
-	-	15-19	374.9	25-29	450.0	35-39	375.5	258.9	375.5	258.9
-	-	20-24	835.6	30-34	399.9	40-44	346.7	254.6	346.7	254.6
15-19	435.0	25-29	709.0	35-39	399.6	45-49	344.2	261.8	344.2	261.8
20-24	778.4	30-34	574.0	40-44	354.0	50-54	292.4	241.2	292.4	241.2
25-29	655.4	35-39	508.8	45-49	320.7	55-59	246.0	199.0	246.0	199.0
30-34	548.7	40-44	439.6	50-54	289.0	60-64	177.4	164.9	177.4	164.9
35-39	571.3	45-49	431.2	55-59	250.6	65-69	102.1	100.5	102.1	100.5
40-44	506.6	50-54	380.8	60-64	206.1	70-74	20.7	43.7	20.7	43.7
45-49	461.0	55-59	312.8	65-69	122.7	-	-	-	-	-
50-54	371.6	60-64	204.4	70-74	44.9	-	-	-	-	-
55-59	269.1	65-69	117.2	-	-	-	-	-	-	-
60-64	195.8	70-74	15.0	-	-	-	-	-	-	-
65-69	123.7	-	-	-	-	-	-	-	-	-
70-74	58.7	-	-	-	-	-	-	-	-	-
Total	4975.3	Total	4903.3	Total	3681.4	Total	4174.5	3150.4	4061.8	3068.8

APPENDIX TABLE 2
NEW ENTRY RATES INTO MALE WORKING FORCE
(AGE AS OF BEGINNING OF DECADE)
BY OCCUPATION AND AGE,
1930-40 AND 1940-50

Occupation	5 to 9 years	
	1930-40	1940-50
Professional, technical and kindred workers	.0032	.0072
Farmers and farm managers	.0085	.0121
Managers, officials and proprietors, except farm	.0018	.0037
Clerical and kindred workers	.0207	.0290
Sales workers	.0244	.0391
Craftsmen, foremen and kindred workers	.0154	.0250
Operatives and kindred workers	.0606	.0856
Service workers	.0216	.0323
Farm laborers and foremen	.1350	.1152
Laborers except farm and mine	.0609	.0592
All occupations	.3521	.4084
Not in civilian working force[a]	.6479	.5916
Total population	1.0000	1.0000
Number not in civilian working force (in thousands)	6,180.1	5,311.3

a. Surviving to end of decade.

APPENDIX TABLE 3
RETIREMENT RATES FROM MALE WORKING FORCE
(AGE AS OF BEGINNING OF DECADE)
BY OCCUPATION AND AGE,
1930-40 AND 1940-50

Occupation	45 to 49 years	
	1930-40	1940-50
Professional, technical and kindred workers	.0115	.0013
Farmers and farm managers	.0119	.0368
Managers, officials and proprietors, except farm	.0262	-
Clerical and kindred workers	.0226	-
Sales workers	.0284	.0116
Craftsmen, foremen and kindred workers	.0072	.0032
Operatives and kindred workers	.0182	.0173
Service workers	-	-
Farm laborers and foremen	.0199	.0466
Laborers except farm and mine	.0289	.0479
Total	.0170	.0162

10 to 14 years		15 to 19 years		20 to 24 years	
·30-40	1940-50	1930-40	1940-50	1930-40	1940-50
.0270	.0311	.0579	.0572	.0642	.0634
.0460	.0335	.0924	.0568	.0874	.0450
.0172	.0181	.0447	.0356	.0635	.0464
.0663	.0651	.0572	.0736	.0067	.0250
.0508	.0479	.0541	.0452	.0346	.0233
.0733	.0915	.1354	.1318	.1025	.1010
.1905	.1938	.2006	.2238	.1232	.1083
.0417	.0373	.0435	.0283	.0387	.0092
.1792	.1361	.0568	.0505	-	-
.1442	.1030	.1351	.0993	.0338	.0102
.8362	.7574	.8777	.8021	.5546	.4318
.1638	.2426	.1223	.1979	.4454	.5682
1.0000	1.0000	1.0000	1.0000	1.0000	1.0000
588.4	5,544.4	2,856.1	3,831.3	568.7	860.2

5 to 49 years		50 to 54 years		55 to 59 years		60 to 64 years	
0-40	1940-50	1930-40	1940-50	1930-40	1940-50	1930-40	1940-50
585	.0049	.0832	.0670	.2544	.2682	.4026	.4130
464	.0559	.1060	.1794	.2313	.3132	.3648	.4747
163	.0114	.2255	.1295	.4201	.3197	.4830	.5042
986	-	.0995	.0387	.4275	.3144	.6730	.5242
009	.0409	.2116	.0761	.4170	.2264	.5208	.4425
757	.0158	.1940	.0752	.4435	.3559	.6828	.6149
886	.0055	.2130	.0719	.4603	.3516	.6867	.6148
-	-	.0160	.0044	.2091	.0900	.4362	.2950
530	.1106	.1885	.1802	.3859	.2815	.6896	.4295
835	.0924	.2567	.2158	.4590	.4675	.8464	.6757
744	.0306	.1705	.1126	.3632	.3219	.5533	.5202